How the World came to Oxford

Refugee stories past and present

Rory Carnegie and Nikki van der Gaag

How the World came to Oxford

Refugee stories past and present

Rory Carnegie and Nikki van der Gaag

How the World came to Oxford
Refugee stories past and present

Design by Alan Hughes.

British Library Cataloguing-in-Publication Data.
A catalogue record for this book is available from the British Library.

ISBN 10: 1-904456-82-0
ISBN 13: 978-1904456-82-7

Contents

Acknowledgments

The authors would like to thank all the young people who participated in the writing and photography projects over the last four years, and the many older refugees who gave of their time and opened their hearts so freely.

We would also like to thank Angie Prysor Jones of The Oxford Literary Festival Charitable Trust for her support and advice over the years; Mercedes Cumberbatch and the staff and trustees of Asylum Welcome; Amanda Webb Johnson of Refugee Resource; Andrew Nairne and the staff at Modern Art Oxford; Oxford University Press; Alan Hughes for his design; and Maggie Black for starting the whole thing off in the first place.

We would like to thank the funders of the book and of last year's exhibition, Arts Council England, Refugee Resource and the Tolkien Trust. This book has been kindly printed by Oxuniprint, Oxford University Press

This book is dedicated to all those who have been, or are refugees in the world today.

Foreword

I FIRST SAW Rory Carnegie's photographs of young asylum seekers a couple of years ago at Modern Art Oxford. I have no memory of the rest of the exhibition, but those six photographs have been floating around the back of my mind ever since.

They're included here (Albert, Amina, Behar, Daphne, Florence and Vassan) and you can probably see why I've found them difficult to forget.

It's due, in part, to the way Rory photographed them. But, more importantly, it's due to the way they look back at him. And at us.

They're self-possessed, yet vulnerable at the same time. They sit in empty rooms, or stand in featureless gardens where nothing happens, but the threat of something hangs in the air.

You can see what I mean when you compare them with the pictures of some of the older people in this book. Mohamed Bishara, for example, or Annelie Rookwood. Time has slowed down in these photographs. The rooms are full of objects. These are people at home with themselves and with the world around them.

When you read the stories they have told to Nikki van der Gaag, you begin to understand why the photographs are so powerful.

Becoming an asylum seeker is not something that happens to people by accident. We talk of people being forced to flee persecution in their home countries. But the brutal truth is that no-one is forced to flee. Fleeing is what you do if you have the guts to leave.

Most people stay and hope for the best. But the best rarely happens. If they're lucky, they lie awake at night waiting for the knock on the door. If they're unlucky they're killed, or tortured, or thrown into prison.

That's the self-possession you can see in these faces. These are people who had the strength to do something most people are incapable of doing: leaving everything behind and starting their lives all over again in a country that often makes this very difficult indeed.

Read the testimonies and you will understand the vulnerability, too. Some of these people have seen their families, friends and neighbours killed.

Look how empty the houses of the younger refugees are, and how few possessions these people have. A book. A football. A flag. A patterned throw. These are people who are fearful of putting down roots, in case they have to move on again at a moment's notice. See how much more at ease they are indoors, but how they still keep the curtains closed so that no-one knows they are in there.

Then notice how these things change as the years pass, as people get older, as they turn from asylum seekers into refugees, and from refugees into people who no longer think of themselves as refugees.

For this is the heart of the book.

Most people are wary of strangers. Tabloid newspapers have always sought to whip that wariness into fear. And governments, in turn, have always used that fear to win votes.

But time does its usual work. Wariness fades, newspapers get bored and it takes a great deal of effort to carry on being frightened of something that offers no threat.

In 50 years' time, it will be unremarkable to have a grandmother who escaped from Rwanda or the former Yugoslavia. Just as it is unremarkable now to have a grandfather who escaped from Nazi Germany.

And this has always been true. If you think you have no refugees in your family it is because you have not looked hard enough, or because the records have not been kept.

This is not a book about how refugees are human beings just like the rest of us. Most of them have had experiences the rest of us cannot even begin to comprehend.

It is a book about how some extraordinary people become an important part of who we all are. ∎

Mark Haddon

Introduction

I wish I had time to tell
My entire story to somebody
Somebody who listens
Really listens
To what I went through

Is there anybody to listen?
Yes.
You who read
Feel it
You
Reach what I went through

It is not a lie. It is true.

Ali Askari, from Afghanistan, published in *The story of my life: refugees writing in Oxford*, edited by Carole Angier (The Charlbury Press 2005).

THE STORY OF this book began in Oxford five years ago, when Rory Carnegie and I were asked to take part in a writing and photography project with young refugees and asylum seekers as part of the Oxford Literary Festival. The project aimed to give the young people some new skills and to build their confidence. It would also help combat some of the stereotypes about asylum seekers that were headlines in the tabloid press at the time. From the beginning we were clear with the young people that this was their project. They could choose the subject and, importantly, decide what they wanted to say and what they didn't.

At that time there were around 240 young asylum seekers in Oxford; since then, numbers have dwindled to 72. This reflects the fact that it has become much more difficult to seek asylum in the UK – applications have fallen by three quarters over the last three years as the system has become more complex and more draconian. Today, the UK is home to just three per cent of the world's refugees – 289,100 out of nearly 9.2 million worldwide.

Most asylum seekers arrive knowing nothing of how the asylum and immigration system works. Often they do not speak English. They are simply trying to escape persecution or conflict in their home countries. They are often surprised and shocked by how they are treated. Adult asylum seekers, for example, are not allowed to work for the first 12 months of their application. They are forced to rely on state support, which is set at just 70 per cent of income support. Many are locked up. Often they wait for years before the Home Office decides their case. As Shami Chakrabarti of Liberty said in a recent Oxford Amnesty lecture: 'We punish those seeking refuge so as to deter others from doing the same.'

However different their stories, refugees under 18 share common experiences when they arrive here. They arrive alone, often having lost their families as well as their homes and friends; they are looked after by Social Services (now the Children, Young People and Families Directorate), sometimes the police; they often live in a bare room in a shared house with other asylum seekers from different countries. There is the struggle to learn English; to cook, sometimes for the first time; to budget and shop for food; to make friends; to study. Then they face the complications of the British legal system. At first they may feel isolated, sometimes depressed. Behar walked up and down Chester Street because it was straight and he knew he would not get lost. Ali raced down the stairs when he finally heard someone speaking Dari, his language, after months of having no-one to talk to.

Over the years of the writing and photography project we got to know a number of the young people well. It seems a long time since we first met a group of young men in the offices of Asylum Welcome, a local refugee support organisation, where they belonged to a youth group. No-one knew quite what to expect; few of the young refugees spoke much English. But we agreed that they were keen to take photos and that the theme they were all most interested in following was their own view of the city that had become their home.

In the weeks that followed they tramped the streets of Oxford with Rory. They enjoyed seeing parts of the city that they had never visited before, and learning to use a camera. They also enjoyed pointing out what they liked best – whether people, buildings or simply green spaces. By the end of the process they all had a good idea of the subjects they wanted to photograph. At the beginning it was Rory who asked people if they minded having their photos taken, but often by the end the young men had the confidence to ask permission themselves. And few people refused them, most responding with a smile.

When the prints came back, we spread them out on my kitchen table and the teenagers chose their favourites and worked on simple captions. We called it: *Picturing Oxford – the City through the Eyes of Young Asylum Seekers*. It was exhibited at Modern Art Oxford and featured in the Oxford Mail and the Oxford Times. Perhaps the best part for us was when the young men saw the quality and professionalism of what they had produced on the walls of one of Oxford's most prestigious museums. Their confidence grew visibly.

The following year we worked with a group of young women who were also part of Asylum

Welcome's youth group. More wary of going outside, and not wanting to be spotted by friends or people who might know them, they decided to focus on fashion and identity and take photos in each other's houses. They dressed up and took photos of each other. Some wore traditional dress, others party clothes. They swathed themselves in sheets and scarves and pretended to be Tony Blair and George Bush. They talked about what wearing certain clothes – like a hijab – meant to them. They wrote about what it meant to be alone in a strange country where you didn't speak the language. They outlined their ambitions to be nurses, doctors, computer technicians and teachers. They had a ball, and so did we.

The third year we worked with both young men and young women. This time they all spoke good English, so we were able to explore more complex ideas and they came up with the idea of looking at their journeys – either physical, spiritual or metaphorical. Some of the young people chose to begin their stories at the point they arrived in Oxford. The past was a country they wanted to forget. Others wanted to start with the land of their birth. For some, the journey was a more metaphorical one: from darkness to light, sorrow to joy.

For many, Oxford also offered hope: the possibility of building a new life, making friends, studying for a different future. They talked of the crucial support given by particular people within Social Services, or Asylum Welcome. 'Oxford is my home now' was a common refrain. It expressed a hope for the end of journeying, but also a fear that their journey would take them back where they came from, away from the life they had so gingerly established for themselves. And they had good reason to be afraid: some of the young people in this book have since been deported and we do not know what has become of them. One simply disappeared, afraid that he would be sent back to his death.

The fourth year we decided to try something new: to continue to work with young refugees but also to talk to those who had come to Oxford as refugees fleeing persecution 10, 20, even 50 years ago and made the city their home. How were their stories different from those of more recent refugees? Were they treated differently? How easy had it been to establish themselves here and to make a living, make a life? The exhibition at Modern Art Oxford that year had a new feel about it, combining the work of the young refugees with interviews and photographs of some of their older counterparts.

With the idea of a book in mind and funding from the Arts Council, the Tolkien Trust and Refugee Resource, a local refugee support organisation, and help from the Oxford University Press, we started to look for people from all over the world who had come to Oxford fleeing persecution in their home countries. They were difficult to identify, as they had melted into the general population. But gradually we explored our networks. We found an artist from Sudan, a doctor from Colombia, a businesswoman from former Yugoslavia, a philosopher from Poland, and many others who were prepared to open their hearts to us. With all those we spoke to, we found that perhaps because of what they had been through and where they had come from, they had come with the same fierce desire as their younger counterparts, to adopt and adapt to their new home and to make something of their new lives. Interestingly, they have made exactly the kind of success of their lives their younger counterparts dream of. Many have equally harrowing stories to tell. Each would make a book on its own.

Over the five years of the project, we talked to many people who decided not to participate in the project because they thought that any publicity might damage their case. They all had good reason to fear the authorities, both in their home countries and in the UK. We were not able to talk to any asylum seekers detained in Campsfield, the main detention centre near Kidlington. Nor did any destitute asylum seekers – those whose cases have been refused and who quite simply have nothing to live on – want to speak about themselves, for fear of being identified. And some who had been refugees many years ago felt too settled here as British citizens to want publicly to trawl their memories of the past.

While respecting the many good reasons for not participating, we also want to acknowledge the many people, young and old, who did agree to be in this book and in the exhibitions; they decided that the necessity of telling their story was greater than any fears they might have about being identified.

All profits from the sale of this book will go to Asylum Welcome and Refugee Resource, to help them continue their work in the community.

Whether they have been here for five weeks or 50 years, all the people in this book, and in the four exhibitions that preceded it, have made a unique contribution to our 'city of dreaming spires'. And it is our hope that they will find an audience, in Ali Askari's words, who will 'listen, really listen' to their stories and enjoy the richness, humour and joy that they bring to our world. ∎

Nikki van der Gaag
nikkivdg@yahoo.co.uk

Ali Askari
Afghanistan

"I walked until my feet were swollen and my knees hurt. Often we had to eat grass. Even now, in the cold, my knees ache."

I AM NOT very old but I feel I have the experience of an old man. I come from a village called Pishighar, which means 'the village in front of the caves'. It is surrounded by mountains, not far from the Bamyan caves where the Taliban blew up the giant Buddhas. My father was an army commander. My mum died when I was seven, so I was brought up by my granddad. My sister married an Iranian and moved to Iran and we never heard from her after that.

In Afghanistan there are four main groups: the Pushtun, the Tajik, the Uzbek and the Hazara. I am Hazara. The Hazara people came from Mongolia about 2,000 years ago, which is why people think I look Chinese. The Hazara people have been treated badly by the others, especially the ruling Pushtun, for 250 years. This is partly the fault of the British, but that is another story.

In the year 2000, when I was 15 years old, the Taliban killed my father. As the son of the commander, I was in grave danger. My grandfather sold our land to send me out of the country. He stayed. He said as an old man he had nothing to lose but his life. The day I left, there were rumours that the Taliban was coming.

We walked through the mountains for two months. I lived with the cows, sleeping in stables or on the ground. I walked until my feet were swollen and my knees hurt. Often we had to eat grass. Sometimes we had to walk waist-deep in water. Even now, in the cold, my knees ache. I had led a very sheltered life in many ways; I wasn't used to hardship.

Finally we stopped walking. We were taken in many lorries, by many different people. I had no idea where we were. I travelled like this for nine months. When I arrived in Oxford, it was not easy at first. I did not speak English. For two or three months I still felt as though I was imprisoned. I had bad dreams. But I made friends, learned English, and passed my exams.

But then I got a refusal letter. It said that because the Taliban were no longer in my country I was not allowed to stay. I was very depressed after that. I left college for a while. I knew that if I went back to Afghanistan there would be people in my village who supported the Taliban, who would want to kill me. Besides, I have nothing to go back to: no family; no land, nothing.

I am waiting for the results of my appeal. I am sick of not having an identity. In Afghanistan the Hazara feel like non-people. As an asylum seeker here you also have no identity; you are always waiting. I want to be recognised as belonging; to be able to make my contribution. I want to stay here and finish my studies. Then I can go back to my country and say 'Enough is enough!' Perhaps I can teach the new generation – to help people to learn to do things a different way. ■

Sedhar Chozam, Lady Ball

Tibet

"When our small poverty-stricken group reached Nepal, we had to beg once our few possessions were all sold. I was told by my sister that I was the best beggar from the group!"

I DO NOT remember everything about my escape from Tibet, but I do know that I was very young, about five or six years old. It was in deep winter when I walked over the Himalayas with my older sister, uncle and other people from my birthplace. I remember seeing lots of snow, sleeping in caves and keeping ourselves warm by burning ancient pine trees.

When our small poverty-stricken group reached Nepal, we had to beg once our few possessions were all sold. I was told by my sister that I was the best beggar from the group! Today I still beg for any help I can get for the people in this very remote and beautiful part of Tibet. It is in a restricted part of the country where there is no education, medication, or everyday needs like tap water, electricity and hygiene facilities. The nomads desperately need help with alternative energy like hydroelectricity, solar or wind energy. At the moment they depend on the sparse shrubs and *yak* dung for fuel.

From Nepal we went by truck to Dharamsala, north of India. Dharamsala is the main base of Tibetan exiles and home to the Dalai Lama.

In 1964, along with three other Tibetan orphans, I started my formal education at Dr Graham's Homes school in Kalimpong. The school was founded in 1900 for Anglo-Indian children. Following the arrival of Tibetan refugees in the early 1960s, international concern resulted in relief aid and sponsorship schemes for education. I was one of the lucky ones to tap into this goodwill. Sheila Stanton, who worked for the National Trust, Rotary club of Sorrento, Victoria and Mrs Eleanor Maltini from Milan were my sponsors.

During the long winter holidays from school, Kalsang, another Tibetan girl and I went to the tea gardens to stay with our foster parents, Yvonne and Clive Robertson. We had to call all the adults Aunty and Uncle. We were brought up amid the dazzling social life at the tail end of the British Raj. Even though I was in India, life at school and at home in the tea gardens could not have been more British.

They have re-married but I still have a very strong bond with them.

My house Aunty at school was a Scottish lady called Jean Burns. She worked at the school for 45 years. She will be 90 years old this year. Aunty Jean came to Buckingham Palace when my husband, John Ball, received his knighthood. She is loved by all the girls she cared for.

As a teenager I fell for the theatre. Felicity Kendall's parents used to come to perform at our school. The school drama club was run by Mrs Webster who came from Scotland. I had a lead role in *Campbell of Kilmore*. Ian Graham, Dr Graham's great grandson, came from England and directed *The Crucible*.

I was the girl's school captain in my last year. I left school in 1974 and every now and then we have a reunion in Kalimpong.

Dr Minto, the school principal from Scotland, invited me to do nursing in Edinburgh. Before going to Scotland, I accepted an invitation to study in Australia for a year. I stayed with members of the Rotary Club of Sorrento. Everyone was so kind and friendly. It was a real culture shock... so much freedom at the school. I keep in touch with my friends from those happy days. I have been fortunate to take my family to meet the families in Sorrento.

Meanwhile, the school principal had got in touch with the Director of Nursing at Western General Hospital in Scotland and I had a place without sitting for an exam. At the time, the UK was happy to give visas to people who wanted to come and train as medical practitioners.

After I had completed my nurse's training in Edinburgh I worked as a nurse for a few years. I then had the opportunity to do a three-year diploma in drama and speech at Queen Margaret University. It was at drama school that I had this burning desire to find out my roots. In acting you have to be able to expose yourself. I needed to know more about my background, and far from being ashamed I knew

that if I learnt more about my roots, the happier and stronger I would be.

When I finished drama school I got an equity card from Newcastle Playhouse to be in a production of *Made in Bangkok* by Anthony Mingella. It was the start of my acting career, that took me from Coventry to Chester to London. I was part of the publicity - people were curious to see a Tibetan acting. I also did TV work in productions such as *EastEnders* and *Take the High Road*.

Then I met my future husband, John, and we travelled together to India. I wanted to show him where I had grown up and to trace my roots. I hadn't seen my sister since we met briefly before I went to Australia, when she insisted that I had an audience with the Dalai Lama before I travelled. I did, but that is another story...

So in 1990 I went to this Tibetan settlement with John. It was very silent, with dim lights flickering in the houses. We asked for my family and the taxi drove us down a dirt track. Then out of the dark someone appeared joyously. It was my brother! He said hello and then to our astonishment, disappeared back into the dark. He was calling everyone else to come out. We stayed up until two in the morning, talking about what had happened. John was amazed how alike my sister and I were, not just to look at, but in our mannerisms and everything. He kept looking from one to the other in amazement.

Since moving to Oxford 10 years ago I have devoted my time to my young family and my husband. The two main causes that are close to my heart are finding sponsors for needy children to study at Dr Graham's School and fundraising for the nomads in Tibet.

As a family, we have visited my birthplace in Tibet in 2002 with my sister and brother. They found the trip very emotional as both of them had lots of memories, unlike me. I felt that our mother was smiling down at us when we reached our ruined house; we held hands and just cried and cried. We left our home this time united and our hearts lighter.

In 2005 we took some aid to the nomads. It takes a day and half on horseback at an altitude of 5,000 metres. The landscape is breathtaking. What I remember is the natural sound of the wind and the tinkling sound of the bells around the horse's neck as it trotted in the wilderness. Sometimes I cried because the sheer peace of mind was too much. I have no relatives in Tibet but my dream is to give humanitarian aid to Tibetans in Tibet as much as I can. Without the support from my husband and his colleagues in China, these journeys would not be possible.

This spring the Dr Graham's Homes choir is touring the UK, with their wonderful singing and I am helping to organise this together with other members of the UK, Dr Graham's Homes committee. Many people have helped to organise this trip. They will sing at St. Paul's church, Covent Garden and at St Andrew's Church, Oxford. I am overwhelmed with the kindness I have seen throughout my life. Now it's my turn to pay back. ■

Said

Somalia

MY NAME IS Said. I am 18 and from Somalia. I have been in Oxford for three years and I am studying business enterprises at Oxford and Cherwell college. When I came here I didn't speak any English. That was hard, but I learned quickly. I like it here – apart from the weather! I have lots of friends, although there are not many people in Oxford from Somalia. I especially like doing horticulture in college – we have an allotment and I want to grow herbs and salad.

I do sport, especially basketball, although I think it is difficult if you come from another country and you have a talent, it is not easy to be recognised. I miss my family and friends. I think life here is too stressed – everyone is always running around, in a hurry to be places on time. ∎

"I miss my family and friends. I think life here is too stressed – everyone is always running around, in a hurry to be places on time."

Professor Brus

Poland

"Germans didn't recognise if you were Jewish or not, but local people would point it out. In the bread queue, even a small 10-year-old boy could point out that you were Jewish and you wouldn't get any bread."

DO YOU KNOW the Chinese curse 'May you live in interesting times'? Well, I have lived in interesting times. If I hadn't spent the Second World War in Russia, I wouldn't be here to be talking to you now. In 1939 Poland was partitioned. My family stayed in Warsaw – but then the Germans entered and after three weeks under German occupation I realised there was no future for me there. Germans didn't recognise if you were Jewish or not, but local people would point it out. In the bread queue, even a small 10-year-old boy could point out that you were Jewish, and you wouldn't get any bread.

We didn't anticipate the Holocaust, but I decided to cross into the eastern part of Poland. I spent two years in Lvov. Then the Germans came again and I walked 600 kilometres further east – my strategy was to keep at least six hours ahead of the Germans. I was with my present wife, but when the Germans attacked in 1941 we were separated. I went deep into Russia by myself and she returned to Warsaw to be with her family. She had to bribe her way into the ghetto and became a member of the underground movement. In 1942 she was ordered to climb over the wall between the Jewish and Catholic cemeteries and she worked with the Aryan underground.

All this time I had no news of her or of my family. When the Polish army was formed in Russia I came back – I left in 1942 before Stalingrad. I returned to Poland in 1944 and took part in a major offensive. In Warsaw I was taken into the political department of the army – there were very few people there with degrees who could do this kind of work. I discovered that my family had all perished. I am sad now that my children never saw their grandparents.

I had met my wife again for two weeks in Eastern Poland, but it didn't work out and I married again and had two daughters. But then I divorced my second wife and married the first one again and had a son – so she is my first wife and my third!

I was at the same university in Poland as Professor Kolakowski, and was one of the other five people to be dismissed. I still have the official book of censorship somewhere – those in the book were banned from writing – our names were not allowed to be mentioned except to criticise us.

The background to all this goes back to 1956 when there were significant changes in Eastern Europe after Krushchev's secret speech. We had great hopes that the Polish economic, social and political system would change.

But gradually the University of Warsaw, where I was working, started to go back to the old ways and we couldn't accept this. We became a hotbed of dissidents – we tried to take advantage of any element where there might be some freedom of speech and to make links with the West where we could. I had links with the economics department in Cambridge. I had books published in France and Spain.

By 1966 we could see that the promise of 1956 had led to disappointment. In 1967 came the Six Days' War and many Poles were enthusiastic about the result – there was a slogan 'Our Jews have beaten the Soviet Arabs!' But the Polish Government was against it and started to play an anti-Semitic card. In 1968 students put on a play by Adam Mickiewicz, Poland's greatest poet, which had been written at the beginning of the 19th century and had a strong anti-Russian element. There were strong reactions from the Government and the students which eventually led to our dismissal.

I was in the economics department at Warsaw at the time. It was not just the professors who were dismissed, but whole departments were closed down because apparently we were spreading corrupt ideologies.

Students also lost their places and had to reapply – most did. But staff were dismissed. Kolakowski was the main villain – we were dismissed in a blaze of publicity. There was a big speech made by the leader of the Polish Communist Party – at one stage I thought I had secured my place in history – but to my chagrin two years later that same leader was

dismissed for presiding over a bloody conflict on the Baltic coast.

Four of the six professors left Poland almost immediately, but I stayed on. I couldn't get a job without the permission of the Central Committee, who assigned me some work in the housing department. I am stupid and stubborn and I never thought I would leave.

But then my son became ill and I was offered a post at the university of Glasgow teaching in my field - the economies of communist countries. The Polish authorities were interested in getting rid of us. So we left. I had a job permit, and left legally, but nonetheless all my academic notes that I had taken with me were confiscated, though they were later returned to me.

From Glasgow I went to St Anthony's College here in Oxford and after two years got a permanent position. I also got permanent unlimited leave to stay here - we later applied for British citizenship. I remember we had to sign a statement of loyalty.

I was welcomed in academic circles. During the hard times in Poland people here were very friendly. I remember there was an Oxford College Hospitality Scheme for Polish students, which each year welcomed a group of Poles, some of whom then went home and some stayed on.

However, couldn't go back to Poland before the system changed - I would have had to surrender my passport and would never have been sure that I could get it back. I visited Poland for the first time in 1989 as part of an agreement between Oxford and Krakow universities. I went back a second time later on, invited by my former department, who offered me back my job, but I didn't see any point in going back after such a long time.

Since October 2005 there has been a new government which is not to my liking - ultra-nationalist, ultra-Catholic, so it is a good thing I stayed. I keep in touch with what is going on in Poland - I read three Polish weeklies - but I feel that I am British.

My life today is between Summertown and the Covered Market. It is not easy getting up all the stairs to our apartment. We have been renting it for over 30 years. But no matter, in a year or two I will be moving to a more permanent apartment in the sky and will have no need for such things. ∎

Roslyn
Uganda

Aliyu
Nigeria

I AM 16. I am from Kano in Nigeria. I have been in Oxford for one month. At first it was very hard. I stayed in a house with other young men from different countries. None of them spoke English, so I couldn't talk to them. Now things are getting better. I am meeting new people and doing a computer course. I have applied to do my A levels.

At first I did the photography project because it was fun. I went with Rory and Albert and visited parts of the city I had never seen before. I enjoyed taking the pictures but didn't think they would be that great. But when I saw them I was blown away – they were really good. I am really pleased with them. ■

"I stayed in a house with other young men from different countries. None of them spoke English, so I couldn't talk to them."

Mldanka Opsenica

Croatia

"It took me seven and a half years to be recognised as a refugee and another three and a half years to become a British citizen."

THE REASON I started my hairdressing business here in Oxford was not in order to be a rich woman, but to say thank you to the British people for what they have given me, to make them look good and feel comfortable. I want to make a contribution to society, to talk to people, to explain that nothing is coincidence, that everything happens for a reason.

I was born in Croatia. I have a degree in chemistry from the university. I am Orthodox, which made me one of a minority in Catholic Croatia, but a minority that had been there for more than 500 years.

I had lovely life as a child. My family didn't get involved in politics. But after President Tito of Yugoslavia died in 1980, things started going wrong.

When the war started in 1991 I was living at the seaside with my brother and my son, who was then four years old. We didn't really believe it was war, but moved to be with my parents in Krajina. My sister was a medical worker – she was ordered to the frontline but she escaped. My brother, however, was not allowed to leave the place where he lived. We couldn't have any contact with him as the telephone lines were cut.

My uncle had lived in England since 1947 and was a British citizen, and he invited us to stay with him. My sister went, but my parents wouldn't leave and I didn't want to leave them on their own. So I stayed, aware that I was staying in a war. Times were tough. We spent six months in a shelter living on bread and apples. I remember going across the frontline to try and find my brother – I went with my son, and just a few hours earlier there had been heavy fighting. There were soldiers standing there and I realised they could shoot us at any point and no-one would be able to do anything. When I think about what I have been through, I don't know how I had the strength. I prayed a lot; I just prayed: 'Please God, let me get through the war.' Maybe I got it from my grandfather, who was a businessman who was killed aged 46 in the Second World War.

After a year my mother decided to send me to Serbia – the war had not started there yet. I got on a bus with my son and said goodbye to my parents. I didn't realise at the time that I would not go back for such a long time. I was a refugee in Serbia for one year. I was treated very badly. I managed to find a job in a café/bar. My intuition helped me through. I also worked as a medium, and many important political people came to see me. I never asked for money, but people paid me anyway. I had very little contact with my parents, though my mother did manage to get through once and we were very sad when realised we didn't know when we would see each other again.

Then my sister called and asked me to come to England. I decided to go. I had no documents, so it took a long time, but I had a friend who spoke good English and he got me a visa even though this was very difficult.

So I came to Oxford, where my uncle was living. I was told that I should apply for asylum – I didn't know what this was. Neither me nor my son spoke English at all. He picked it up very quickly and is now at university in London. I went to college for three years to learn English. But then I couldn't find a job in chemistry so I decided to change my career. I had always been good at hairdressing, so I did a two-year course and I won first prize in the first year!

I had a job as a hairdresser in this very salon, but the lady who owned it treated me very badly so I took her to court and won my case of racial discrimination and bullying. I went to another salon for two years and then someone told me that the woman who owned this place had gone bankrupt. I was looking for a place but never dreamed that it would be here in the same salon!

In the meantime the war went on in Croatia. In 1995 the army pushed 400,000 people out of Krajina in one single day, including my parents. They had to leave everything behind, from a needle to an animal. We had no news of them for 11 days. Then we heard that they were ok, that they were refugees in Serbia. We applied to bring them here – three times they were refused, but on the fourth attempt we succeeded. We found my brother too and brought him here. The day after he arrived he heard that he had been called up to the Croatian army, so we probably saved his life. My family were now reunited.

It took me seven and a half years to be recognised as a refugee and another three and a half years to become a British citizen, although I had had permission to work after six months. For 10 years I was a citizen of nowhere. Finally I approached my MP and the answer came within two weeks – it was yes!

Last year I went back to Croatia to face the reality of my past. Everything was smashed and stolen. Our house was razed to the ground. My childhood had been destroyed. It was hard, but I am glad I went back. I found that I did not hate the people who had done this – you can't hate all Croatians because of the decisions of a few political people. I persuaded my father to go too, and he was released after seeing it all.

During a war like the one we went through, you just concentrate on surviving. You have to keep going, and God gave me the strength to stand up again every time I was knocked down. I would like to thank all the many people who helped me – there will never be enough words to say thank you to them. Somehow the right people came at the right time. If you hate people, that is what will come back to you. But if you respect them, you will earn their respect. ■

Daphne
Rwanda/Uganda

"Although the things that happened to me were dreadful, I do not regret it because now I stand strong and proud, doing the things that I have always wanted to do."

DON'T EXPECT ROSES; it's been tough but worthwhile. My name is Daphne; I am 21. I was born in Rwanda in central Africa but grew up in Uganda until the age of 16 when I came to the UK. I am currently studying a higher national diploma in business management and accountancy which I hope to transform into a degree come September this year.

To get to where I am, it has been a long journey. Having lost my family at a very tender age, I had to start fending for myself. I have met various kinds of people in this journey through life. Some have failed and disappointed me, while others have helped me turn my life into something worth living for.

However, I could not do this until I found it in my heart to forgive the people who had wronged me. It was not easy, but with a lot of spiritual guidance, a network of great friends and a new-found self belief, I did it.

Growing up in a country where not much attention is paid to the rights of children or their vulnerability, it was tough to keep on the right track and uphold my morals and beliefs. People treated me as they pleased because I was vulnerable and had no way out. I was shouted at, beaten, abandoned and mistreated. They made me believe that I deserved all the things that were happening to me. There was no escape because they were either teachers or guardians, whose help and guidance I needed if I was to become someone in this world.

I did not have it easy even when I came to the UK. There were people here who also treated me badly. The first months were very gloomy. I lived in fear and frustration, not knowing what was going to happen to me next. I felt disorientated. In my heart, I think I had given up on life.

Then, in August 2001, I met my very dear friend Dawn Little. She was assigned to me as a social worker. I thank God every day that I met her at that point in my life. She believed in me when no-one else did. She made me realise that this was not the end. She helped me to see that I had been given a chance to start over. Because she believed in me, I also started to believe in myself.

Now my demons do not laugh at me anymore. I have control over my life. Although the things that happened to me were dreadful, I do not regret it because now I stand strong and proud, doing the things that I have always wanted to do. Looking back, I thank God for my life. I thank him that when everything was downhill, he sent me an angel who helped me mend my life. ∎

Sister Eugenie

Burma

"But to do this I had to change my identity. I folded my habit very small, changed into civilian clothes and even left my rosary and prayer book behind."

I AM A Burmese nun. My country, Burma, has a Buddhist majority and only 1.8 per cent of the population is Christian, but there are a number of orders of Catholic nuns. In 1990 I was the co-founder of a new order. Our special work was to help the people in remote areas on the borders of our country where there was no electricity, often no doctor or nurse, and illnesses such as malaria. People were very poor and we would train nurses and teachers. My job was to visit the Sisters in these areas and to help them with their work.

One day my superior realised that we needed to have someone who could speak English. So many of the spiritual books we were using were in English rather than Burmese. He asked me if I would go to the UK. I said yes. It was 1996.

The next thing I knew I was travelling on a plane with a novice nun to England. It was both scary and funny at the same time. We were supposed to be met at Heathrow. I had only a few words of English that the superior had taught me. I knew how to read 'arrival' and 'departure', so I followed the arrivals sign and waited. I was so nervous, my body was shaking and I nearly cried. We waited for a long time. Eventually we got through immigration and on the other side a woman rushed up and hugged us. She was not wearing a nun's habit but she recognised ours. I was so happy to see her.

The Sister drove us to Bognor Regis, where she worked with the elderly. We stayed there for a month but there was not much for us to do and it was not a good place to learn English. Our Order was connected to the Salesian Order, and Sister knew there was a Salesian convent in Oxford and that Oxford would be a good place to study English. So our next stop was the Cowley Road, where we were welcomed by the Mother Superior.

After a couple of days she called me and asked how much money I had for our studies. I only had $100! I think she was rather surprised. I knew that my superior was coming to Rome the following week and so I said I would speak to him then. In the meantime, we were welcome to stay at the convent. We had one hour's English lessons a day, although I knew this was not enough. I felt really homesick. I couldn't eat the food – I was used to rice not bread – and filled up with water at night so I was hungry all the time.

One day a man came to the convent. He was surprised to meet two Burmese nuns because he too had a connection with Burma. A week later he invited us to his home to cook Burmese food. It was a visit that was to change my life.

Not long after this we received an invitation – would we come and live in his house, cook for him and look after his child? In return, he would pay for English lessons for us. It was only when we went to his house that I saw the photos of Aung San Suu Kyi. There was little news of her in Burma but of course I knew of her as a famous opposition leader. 'Do you know this person?' I asked. 'She is my wife,' he replied. We stayed there for a year. It was a good time. We went to mass every day at 6.00 pm in the Catholic Church.

In 1999, Uncle Michael, as we called him, died in Oxford. I was very sad. I went back to my mother house in Burma. Later, I heard that he had left me some money to continue my studies in English. I asked my superior if I could go back for a year and he said yes. But to do this I had to change my identity. I folded my habit very small, changed into civilian clothes and even left my rosary and prayer book behind. Only three people knew I was going. Not even the other Sisters or my family knew. My documents had been destroyed. In Burma I was officially dead.

Sitting in the waiting room, waiting for the plane to England, I was very scared. Then my heart beat fast as I saw a man who knew me. It was not good news. He came up and asked me where I was going. I said 'To the Philippines'. Then another man came and asked me more questions. He left too and I waited for 45 minutes. Every minute I thought someone would come for me, but eventually the plane was called and I flew to England.

The man at the airport had not been satisfied and had reported me to the authorities. I could not go back home. Since then, I have been studying English and working for the Parish. I had not seen my parents for seven years but I could manage to see them earlier this year. My father was looking very frail.

I still hope for change in my country. I was very happy when the United Nations Secretary-General went there two months ago. I would like to go home. ■

Behar

Kosovo

"I lost my friend and my bag. I never saw my friend again and I don't know where he is now."

WHEN I FIRST arrived in Oxford I was 16 years old. I became a very quiet person. I used to stay at home all day by myself. I couldn't smile. People used to come up to me and ask me why I was so serious all the time. I didn't like the food – I used to be sick a lot. I didn't speak any English and didn't know anybody.

I came from my home town Mitrovica with a friend. I had a bag of clothes with me. But when we got to Dover it was all very confusing and we got separated by the police into groups. We were given food and told our rights – there was an Albanian translator. Then I went with some other people on a bus to Oxford, where they knew some people. I lost my friend and my bag. I never saw my friend again and I don't know where he is now.

The bus stopped in Headington. I was with a group of other guys from many different countries – Iraq, Afghanistan – and one of the Albanians knew someone in Oxford, so I had a place to stay for a couple of nights. I felt very alone. I had 100 Euros in my pocket but couldn't change them because I couldn't make anyone understand what I wanted. I didn't know anyone. I was afraid of getting lost so I used to walk up and down Chester Street, near where I lived in East Oxford, because it was a straight street and I knew I could find my way home. I kept looking for people who were Albanian so that I could talk to someone.

After a few days I was in Florence Park playing football with some Albanians I had met and I met a Kosovan family. They had two boys, much younger than me. We started to talk. They had been here for five or six years and they explained to me that I could go to Social Services for help – I didn't know anything about housing or education or benefits. They also said that I could come and live with them if I could sort it out with Social Services. I have been with them ever since. I think they are the only family who has taken an asylum-seeker in to live with them in this way. It has made things much easier for me – I see other young people in my situation being moved around every few weeks, even getting into trouble with the police.

At Social Services I met Dawn. She was very helpful and I could phone her or speak to her with my half-English talk and some sign language! After three or four months I started going to school – my family found out that I could apply to the Community English School for a full-time English course. I was very nervous; worried about being with English people who wouldn't understand me. I had to wait a month.

But when I arrived, there were lots of other refugees too. I stayed for a year and did all the courses in English for beginners. I used to play football with the school in my spare time. Then I found they also had computer courses. I had seen computers in Kosovo but had never used one before. My teacher told me that I was quite good and said maybe I should try and go to college and do a computer course. She has been a great support ever since that time. We still meet regularly for a cup of tea or coffee.

I went first to the Ethnic Minority Business Service and did a number of computer courses. I never missed a class. I did two courses at once and an English class in the evening. My English was now good enough to go to college to do an IT Foundation course. I was really scared – I had to fill in forms, go to lots of interviews; but I was offered a place at the FE College. I was very happy to go to an Oxford college – such a big name! I never had this kind of opportunity in my country – there you have to pay a lot of money to do such a course. The teacher will give the tests and people who may not be very good can still pass if they pay the teacher a lot of money. People like me with no money would never stand a chance.

In college, I made many new friends. One of my good friends was from Libya. I used to play pool with him a lot. But now he has moved to London and I have lost touch with him. I found it easiest to make friends with other Muslims, probably because we share a similar culture. In fact, though I am Muslim by culture, back home I used to go to church with my family and pray on Sundays. So I am a Muslim in some ways and a Christian in others, I suppose. In Kosovo we celebrate New Year rather than Christmas or Eid in any case.

Anyway, I finished my foundation course in computers. By this time I felt comfortable in Oxford. I found out about Asylum Welcome and started getting to know Hana and Jamie and going to their youth club, playing pool, going swimming and eventually even going on holiday with them. The strange thing was that when I was on holiday I was homesick for Oxford!

If I have to go back it will all have been for nothing. I will have to start again in Kosovo just like I had to start over here in Oxford. I have no family left there, no home. There is an Albanian saying: 'Nobody dies for lack of food' in Kosovo. So I won't starve if I have to go. But I want to stay and finish my studies and if possible go to university. I like the life, my family, my friends, college and the possibility to study. Oxford feels like my home now.' ∎

Rita Fatimaharan

Sri Lanka

"We stayed in our neighbour's house for a week – we couldn't eat, drink or sleep. We still didn't know if my younger brother was safe."

I AM SO proud to live here in Oxford. My Sri Lankan friends call me an 'Oxfordtarian'! In my childhood I heard a lot about Oxford University. A lot of our politicians and professionals studied here. But I never thought I would even visit, let alone come to live here or to work and study. I did my BSc and Postgraduate diploma at Oxford Brookes University.

When we first moved to Oxford we didn't know anyone. My husband had come first for his studies and my three children and I missed him so we followed. We are Catholics, and we asked people: 'Where is the nearest church?' From then on things flowed very smoothly. We found a church in Hollow Way, and the parish priest helped us with school admission. We both were able to work and study, though it took some time until we had our official papers. I worked as a language teacher and then a housing officer.

My husband and I are also involved with TTN, the Tamil TV Network, which is based in Paris. During the time of the tsunami I phoned the BBC and asked them why they were only covering the situation in the South, which is mainly Sinhalese, and not in the Tamil north and east of the country, which were even more affected. They said that the Sri Lankan Government only took them to the South. But I knew that Tamils abroad would also be wanting to know what had happened to their loved ones. I gave the Tamil TV Channel phone number to the BBC and asked them to contact them for the footage from the north. The BBC then used this footage.

In general however, if things happen in the Sinhala area it is shown, but in the Tamil area, every day people are killed, raped, are short of baby food and medicine. The Government says they are searching for the Tamil Tigers, but the army tortures Tamil youth until they make false complaints about the Tigers.

Why did I leave my country? It is a long story. In 1983 I had left my hometown of Jaffna in the north and was teaching in St Joseph's College in Colombo, which was a joint Tamil and Sinhala medium school. In Sri Lanka about two thirds of the people are Sinhala and one third Tamil, but the Tamils mostly live in the north and east and the Sinhala in the South.

On 25th July, I was going to the school with my nephew on the bus, and we saw people looking and breaking the windows of Tamil shops. After that we saw people running and crying and lots of smoke. The driver said: 'Don't panic. I'll stop the bus at a safe place.' Finally we arrived at St Joseph's. Parents were taking their children home; teachers were not taking classes. I went up to the second floor and saw fire everywhere. My colleagues came and told me that people with knives were searching for Tamil teachers. They told me to take off my *pottu* – the mark that Tamil women wear on their foreheads to show they are married. Our rector said 'Stay in school'. But my next-door neighbour came to pick up his son. He was a Tamil too, but from India – Sinhalese people accept Indian Tamils but not Sri Lankan Tamils, so he was not in the same danger.

He drove us home, telling us to keep our heads down, and not to look out of the window. But we couldn't help but see the blood, smell the burning and hear the terrible noises of people being killed. One person was dragged off his motorbike and set on fire with petrol from the fuel tank. The people around were clapping and laughing.

We reached home safely, but still didn't know where my two brothers were. One had left for his job with Air Lanka in the morning but had not come home. A few hours later we saw many people in sarongs with weapons outside our area. They were like butchers. They were coming from the slum area towards our house, chanting 'We are going to kill all Jaffna Tamils'. We went out the back door into the next-door neighbour's house. We could hear the sound of windows breaking in our house. Our neighbour told us to stay in one room and that they

would keep us safe. This was very brave of them as the crowd were threatening to kill anyone who kept Jaffna Tamils in their house.

The noise went on from morning until late into the night. My brother, on his way home, was pulled inside by another neighbour and told that it was not safe to go home and where we were. We were so happy to see each other; we had both thought the other might be dead.

We stayed in our neighbour's house for a week – we couldn't eat, drink or sleep. We still didn't know if my younger brother was safe. When we finally went back all the windows had been broken. Another neighbour told us that the mob had climbed over the locked front gate but then seen the Jesus image and the red lamp on the little altar. They heard someone say: 'They are not Hindus – let's leave this house and search elsewhere.' They were mainly searching for Hindus not Christians.

My elder brother then went to search for my younger brother and brother-in-law. In their house, their lunch was still on the table in their room. Everything was scattered. A lady told my brother that she had seen them run and that he should search the temples and churches where the refugees were hiding. He couldn't find them. He drove around hooting the horn of his van and eventually my brother recognised the sound and they were reunited. My brothers cried loudly. They were so happy to see each other.

After that my mother said I should give up my job and come home to Jaffna. I stayed with my parents and in 1984 I got married. But in Jaffna there was also shooting and the army was making trouble for Tamils. I told my husband he should leave; it was not safe for young men. I was nine months pregnant when he left for India.

My son was born and one month later I joined my husband. We were to stay in India for five years. Each year we renewed our visa with the Indian government, but after the fifth year they would no longer renew it. We wanted to go home but my mother said it was not safe. So we came to Britain in 1991.

By now I had two sons. Another was born in the UK. But it took us 10 years to get permanent residence here. The saddest thing was when my mother died five years ago; I couldn't go to her funeral because I was still not allowed to leave the country. The same when my brother died in France. This was a terrible thing. I finally went back two years ago. I had been away for 20 years. It was still not safe for my husband or my sons to go. I hope one day that they will be able to see my country. ■

Vasan
Sri Lanka

Cecilia

Kenya

"It didn't feel too strange coming here because there is so much British influence in Kenya. It is the language of education, of the law and the courts, even of business."

MY NAME IS Cecilia. I am 18. I am from Kenya, and I am studying computers at college. Everyone always says that I look like a Maasai, even though I am not a Maasai but from the Meru tribe. It is because I have this gap in my teeth and long legs – I noticed those in the photos, especially when I am wearing jeans or a skirt.

But then it might come from my great grandmother, who was pure Maasai. The different tribes used to do raids on each other and steal each other's cattle. They sometimes stole girls as well. My great grandfather was one of those raiders, and he took my great grandmother who bore him children... so maybe I look like her.

It didn't feel too strange coming here because there is so much British influence in Kenya. It is the language of education, of the law and the courts, even of business. For example, if people want to be accountants, their papers are sent back to England for examination. But now American influence is coming – everything is becoming American. The shops are full of American stuff, the music is American R and B. We have American clothes, American entertainment and TV. We have a few British programmes – *Men Behaving Badly* and *Mr Bean* – but otherwise it is all American. We get American films there even before you get them here!

Especially in Nairobi, people can no longer speak their mother tongue but only English. This means that you are never sure who you really are, where you are from; the bottom line is this gives you your identity. A friend of mine recently quoted something to me in Swahili and then was shocked when I did not understand him – I speak Swahili, but this was a saying that I didn't understand and he said: 'What are you going to teach your children?' I don't know what will happen with the next generation in Kenya... They may not know their own culture. ∎

Grażnya Cooper

Poland

"The other children decided that Jews walk in a particular way, and I was made to walk through the centre of the classroom with everybody watching."

I CAME TO England nearly 40 years ago because my parents felt they had to protect me from the dangers of the anti-Semitic purge of 1967-68 in Poland. The West was hardly aware of the fact that a million Jews were expelled from my country at that time. Instead, the world was eagerly watching communist Czechoslovakia.

I had always felt there was something different about my family. I remember when I was a child wondering why my family was so small – there was me and my sister and our parents, my grandmother on my mother's side, my father's sister and her family, and my mum's brother, Tad, who was a prominent film-maker at that time. My friends had much larger families. I was 17 before I found out why.

In the meantime, I had a rich and happy childhood. We did lots of cultural things, went to the theatre, ballet and opera, saw as many films as possible, and had lots of friends. I loved Warsaw as a city and can remember its reconstruction. People were very determined to overcome the destruction of 90 per cent of the city by the Germans – and my parents were hugely patriotic Poles.

I was baptised and brought up a Catholic. My grandmother was a very spiritual woman and had a big influence on me. Her Christianity was very important to her and very personal and she encouraged me to understand it. I remember my best friend coercing me gently to go to church every Sunday.

My father was a member of the Communist Party, and though this was partly for career reasons, he was certainly socialist in his beliefs and outlook.

One of my strongest memories comes from when I was seven. For some reason there was a rumour going round the classroom that I was Jewish – despite the fact that I had blue eyes and my parents looked typically 'Aryan'. The other children decided that Jews walk in a particular way, and I was made to walk through the centre of the classroom with everybody watching. In the end,

my classmates decided I wasn't Jewish after all. I remember feeling both relieved and triumphant, thinking even then that somehow I had managed to fool them.

During my school days we had many history lessons about World War Two. There was a lot of awareness in particular of how badly Poland had been treated during the Occupation and of the Warsaw Uprising and the great tragedy of the last days of the war. But very little was said about the fact that many Jewish families had been denounced by Poles, or how the Catholic Church had a track record in Poland in particular of being overtly anti-Semitic. Of course there were many good Poles as well – I remember stories of a Jewish friend who was rescued from the Ghetto and hidden in a wardrobe by a Polish family as a child during the War.

One of my uncles was in the British Army during the Second World War. He was one of the pilots who fought in the Battle of Britain. When he came back in the late 1940s he was arrested and sentenced to death for being a spy. He was in prison under sentence of death until 1956. He was one of many Polish soldiers who had managed to get away to England and who had fought on the Allied side, then elected to come back home to rebuild their country, and were subsequently imprisoned or sentenced to death. Until 1956 we were living in the increasingly terrifying Stalinist era.

My uncle's return and arrest were the end of my father's career in the Polish army. He and my Uncle Tad had both managed to escape to the Soviet Union in 1944 and came back as part of the army that liberated Poland. Tad went to film school when the war ended – along with Wajda, Polanski and the future Pope – but my father became a Major and would probably have gone on to be a General. But my other uncle's imprisonment made the authorities of that time suspect the entire family. For many years we lived in fear that my father would also be arrested. I was too small to understand what was going on, but I certainly sensed the tensions and

unspoken fears that surrounded my family.

Then, mercifully, in 1956 Stalin died. I believe that that saved our country and many others from a period of paranoid insanity. Gradually things eased. My uncle was released. But by then my father had been dismissed from the army. He went back to the university to study economics. He eventually began to build a very successful career in that field internationally, which turned out to be a great help in the future when he was forced to leave his country.

When I was 17, I was looking through my parents' desk and came across some documents stating my parents' religion was Jewish. I began questioning them about it and they finally had to admit to being Jewish. I also discovered that over 50 members of my family had perished in the Holocaust. Once I knew that, I sat my grandmother down and she told me the whole story of my family, their years in hiding, their amazing escapes, their work in the Underground. One story especially haunts me. We had had cousins who lived in Dresden and owned a big department store, and after Hitler came to power and they were being targeted for being Jewish, the entire family committed suicide.

I continued my studies in Warsaw, innocently unaware of the brewing political and economic problems that were about to erupt into a shocking anti-Semitic purge. The economy was in disarray and the Government needed a scapegoat. Many Polish Jews held prominent jobs and, like my Uncle Tad, were quite outspoken about the political climate of that time. Unlike other Communist Eastern block countries, Poles had continued to insist upon and enjoy relative freedoms of speech.

However, because the Government was so frightened of offending the Soviet Union just after the dramatic events in Czechoslovakia, it suddenly banned a famous play, a classic of Polish literature *Dziady*. It was decreed to be anti-Russian. The banning of the play initially sparked off peaceful protests by students that then turned violent following brutal retaliations by the police. The disaffection spread and the Jewish students were blamed.

The Government accused Polish Jews of being pro-Israeli and pro-war in the Middle East. In effect, Jews were declared the enemies of the State. Everyone with even remote Jewish family ties was labelled a Zionist, although at that time I did not even know what the word meant.

The secret service did painstaking research into birth certificates to discover who was of Jewish descent. People who had no idea, because their parents had been, in a sense, in hiding since the German invasion of 1939, suddenly discovered they had Jewish roots. Some of my Polish school friends found themselves in this situation. Suddenly, Poland had one and a half million 'perfidious' Jews among its citizens and there was a real danger of another pogrom.

At this point, Cardinal Wyszynski went on the radio and appealed to the nation for calm and asked if Poles really wanted to repeat the atrocities of just over 20 years before.

My father was interrogated by the Communist Party, stripped of his membership and dismissed from his job. Over a million Polish Jews were given 'permission' to leave Poland for Israel. However, it was the time of the 1967 war and few people wanted to go there.

Vienna became a holding place for displaced Polish Jews from which they were supposed to leave for Israel. Those who did not wish to go to Israel were given, instead, the option of going to places like Sweden and Denmark – which were happy to welcome Jewish intelligentsia, consisting mainly of highly skilled and educated people. My parents went to Denmark, where through work contacts both of them were offered jobs. My sister by then had finished university and was married to a Pole. I was already in England and my parents assumed that I would join them wherever they finally managed to settle.

Through Uncle Tad and his connections in the West, I was living with the family of a Jewish doctor in Hampstead. Dr Parnes was once in one of my uncle's films that he made in Africa for the United Nations. He was also a friend of the secretary of the Duke of Marlborough and he felt I would be better off living in Oxford and attending a good language school in order to improve my English. I was invited by the Duke's secretary to come to Woodstock and found myself living in Blenheim Palace in a room with a four-poster bed overlooking a beautiful lake and a splendid park. It felt as if I was back in feudal times.

I was studying English during the week and working for the Duke at weekends. One of my jobs was to welcome his weekend guests and walk his dogs. I found the palace etiquette stifling – I even refused to address the Duke as 'Your Grace'. I stayed for about six months but increasingly felt distressed by the claustrophobia of the place. I even resorted to barricading my bedroom door every night in fear of being accosted by one of the young Spanish footmen who were relentlessly pursuing me.

My English teacher, Anne Strawson, was aware of my plight and one day she simply got into her Morris Minor, drove to the Palace and told me to pack my bags. I lived with the Strawsons, a highly intellectual family (Peter Strawson was a famous philosopher) for a year. During that time I met my future husband, who was a student at Wadham College, Oxford. He came from an Indian Nawab family. His mother was a politician, a rival of Mrs Gandhi's, and his father was a greatly respected and loved academic.

By this time my parents were living and working in Denmark. However, the Polish Government refused my sister and brother-in-law's application to leave Poland because she was married to a Pole. My brother-in-law was interrogated and accused of betraying Poland for a Jewess. Eventually my then-husband, through his family connections with the Indian embassy in Warsaw, managed to get them a permit to visit us in Oxford, and from here they went to Denmark to join my parents.

I loved England and felt at home here. I found the English congenial, witty and tolerant. Five years after I arrived I was naturalised. I studied computing at Oxford Polytechnic and got my first job in 1979 with the Oxford University Computing Services. By then I had a seven-year-old daughter and had divorced my first husband. In 1980, I married Mel, who is Canadian and also Jewish. His parents were keen for us to marry in a synagogue and that was quite an undertaking as the Orthodox rabbinate, ironically, would not believe I was Jewish! In addition, I had never been to a synagogue.

I have remained a Christian because of my grandmother's influence and because of my upbringing. But I am very interested in my Jewish roots and their contribution to who I am.

I didn't want to go back to Poland for a long time, but since the fall of Communism I have been back a few times. I enjoy the nostalgia and the buzz that I experience in Warsaw and I love seeing my friends.

But I feel British. I have lived longer in Oxford than Warsaw. This is where I have made a career at Oxford University; and this is where I have married and my daughters and granddaughters have been born. This is the place that gave me a refuge at a very tough time in my life and it is now definitely my home. ■

Besmira

Albania

"We were sent to Newcastle. I was one of only two foreign people in the whole school and we were teased and bullied because of this."

MY NAME IS Besmira. I come from Albania, I am 16 years old. I am proud of being Albanian, even though sometimes I am put down because of it. Anyway, it is something I can't change. I have lived in this country for four years, though I have only been in Oxford a few months. I came with my mum and my sister; we had to leave our home because my mum was a single parent and a Catholic. We were living in a Muslim area because my dad, who left when I was very young, was a Muslim. But it was not easy; people used to say horrible things about us. My mum got depressed and me and my sisters had such a hard time at school that eventually we stopped going. That is why I now read and write English better than Albanian.

When we came here we were sent to Newcastle. It wasn't easy there either because I was one of only two foreign people in the whole school and we were teased and bullied because of this. I was friends with the other Albanian, though. She was called Lily. Then one day my mum said I was going to stay with Lily for a couple of weeks. She left with my sisters but never came back. She abandoned me. I didn't know what to do. I had a Kosovan friend in London so I went to stay with her, but because I was only 15 I was sent into a children's care home. It was OK there; I made lots of friends, but then I was sent back to Newcastle to a foster family and that just didn't work out. I didn't fit in. I only had £10 a week; I couldn't go out, go to the cinema, do anything. My solicitor told me I had to stay there but I didn't want to, so I applied to go to Oxford to stay with my mum's friend. I was able to take some stuff from my house – my sister's CD player, some make-up, my computer, but I had no money or anything so she had to feed me and buy me clothes.

She also sent me to Asylum Welcome, where I met Lauren, the youth worker. Lauren really helped me. Now I have my own room, friends, and I am studying business enterprises at Oxford and Cherwell College. People say I look English in the way I dress and speak. Once I had to go to the Home Office with another Albanian – he thought I was from Social Services, not a refugee like him! Some of my beliefs are more English too; I am not going to get married young like Albanians do.

I am proud of what I have done. I have had to do a lot on my own. I don't let people get me down. I want to be an actress when I am older. Or at least to be famous. I don't know if I will succeed, but I am not going to stop trying. ∎

Mohamed Bishara

Sudan

I AM MOHAMED Bishara, an artist from Sudan. I have drawn and painted all my life, using found material such as scraps of paper, wood, coffee, sugar and sand when I had no money for art supplies.

As a young man, I studied at the University of Khartoum in Sudan and then got a British Council scholarship to study printmaking at the Slade School of Fine Art, in London.

When I went back to Sudan, I was head of the Fine Art section at the Department of Culture in the Ministry of Culture and Information in Khartoum. But my art was considered political, and because of the oppressive atmosphere created by the military regime at that time, I left Sudan for Saudi Arabia.

In 1999 my family and I sought asylum in the UK. I was expecting the worst when I arrived at the airport. You have more to worry about when you bring your whole family. But we were treated very well. Lots of people helped us.

When we arrived, we had to find a house, schools for the children, all kinds of things; but it all gradually fell into place. Through a series of coincidences, someone took my CV to Blooming Arts which offered me a small space to work. For the first time in my life I had a space of my own to work in outside my house. It was really special to open that door with my own key every morning.

Most of my art used to be on big canvases or paper, but since I have been in the UK I mainly do small paintings, etchings and collographs. There was simply no room on the kitchen table for large works! I draw whenever and wherever I can, but I have recently been coming back to printmaking.

I see art as a different language: a new way of communicating. For me, art is like archaeology – I know the ideas are there and I am digging for them. Sometimes I find a treasure; sometimes I do not. I start to work from nowhere, without an idea. Then there is a dialogue between the surface and myself. Ideas begin to build up. The more I work, the more things develop until I become in full control of the image.

I am a Member of Oxford Printmakers Co-operative, who gave me their annual award in 2004. I did a workshop last year for refugees in Campsfield House which was very rewarding but also made me sad. I have had many exhibitions – in New York, Los Angeles, Greece, France, Ghana, Eritrea, London and Oxford. I am currently working on material for two exhibitions in France; the 7th World Print Triennale of Small Size Prints and Contemporary and African Printmakers.

I feel very lucky. I never dreamed I would live in such a beautiful city. I feel very appreciative of the art community in Oxford. They welcome me as an artist in my own right, not just a 'Refugee Artist'. It is a privilege to be able to continue my art. It would not be possible in Sudan, while here I can paint, draw and dream of a better world. ∎

"For the first time in my life I had a space of my own to work in outside my house. It was really special to open that door with my own key every morning."

Juli Beattie

Hungary

"When we arrived in England, we were given the 'red carpet treatment'. People bent over backwards to help us."

MY NAME IS Juli Beattie. I am currently the director of The Art Room. The Art Room is a project based in East Oxford that offers art as therapy to some of the most vulnerable children in the community. These are children who may be at risk of exclusion or who are finding it difficult to manage mainstream school.

The project was set up five years ago by me and a group of friends in Oxford. We now cater for up to 50 children and young people a week. The students attend during school hours and are referred by their schools.

Our main aim is to raise the self-esteem and confidence of the young people we work with. We focus exclusively on positive behaviour and achievement. We praise even the smallest success.

I find this work extremely exciting and rewarding. Perhaps it is because of my own background that I have been drawn to working with children who are facing real challenges in their lives.

I escaped from Hungary in December 1956 with my mother, my father and my sister. The Hungarians had rebelled against Soviet rule and the Russian tanks were rolling into Budapest to suppress the revolt. We left Budapest by train. We travelled under the pretext that we were accompanying my grandmother to the border: she had a visa to leave the country and visit my Uncle in England. We could not take any luggage. Instead my mother dressed as all in three layers of clothing each.

We got off the train at a small station on the Hungarian side of the Austrian border, while my grandmother continued her journey to Vienna. I remember my mother saying to her: 'Do not cry; you'll give us away.' It must have been so hard for both of them. There were soldiers on the train and we could have been arrested had they realised that we were trying to escape.

Having left the train, we met a local farmer who said that his son, an off-duty soldier, would take us across the Austrian border, for a fee. By this time 34 other people, all with the same plan, had joined us.

I remember a father cradling his baby. The baby would not stop crying as we made our escape on foot. Some of the people in the group said the baby should be killed, because he was endangering all our lives. My parents were amongst the group who would not allow this to happen.

We walked all night in the December rain. I do not remember being cold, but I do remember being frightened. I remember hallucinating and thinking that the trees around me seemed to have faces.

The border guards were shooting flares into the sky, lighting up the fields around us, to look for people trying to escape. When we heard the whoosh of the flares, we had to lie down in the mud. We were covered in mud by the end of the journey and to this day I do not like the touch of clay or soil on my skin.

After a 10-hour walk the man who had been showing us the way left us, to go back to his home. He told us to walk towards a light that we could see in the distance. This light, he told us, was on Austrian soil.

When we got there, we were met by members of The Austrian Red Cross. That night, after a drink of hot chocolate, we slept in a barn.

The next day we travelled to Vienna where we had an emotional reunion with my grandmother.

In Vienna some cousins put us up in a hotel, but we had no money for food. The chambermaids in the hotel collected the leftovers from the guests' breakfast trays, for us to eat. These maids were the first of many people who were kind to us, despite having very little themselves.

We could have chosen many other countries to live in, but we came to England because my uncle was already here and my father wanted the whole family to be together.

Many countries felt bad that the West was not really prepared to help Hungary because of the Cold War and the Suez Canal.

When we arrived in England, we were given the 'red carpet treatment'. People bent over backwards to help us. I remember one particular woman – who went on to become a very good friend of my mother – who arrived at our flat one day with four suitcases. There was a suitcase for each of us, containing all the things this woman thought we would need to start a fresh life here. There were things like shaving equipment for my father, jewellery and perfume for my mother and toys for me and my sister. She'd even bought a wind-up gramophone for my father because she had heard that he was a music lover.

The husband of this same kind woman offered himself as guarantor at the bank in order that my parents were able to start their own business in London, buying and selling coffee. The shop, Markus Coffee, is still there now, not far from Marble Arch.

Other people brought us gifts when they found out that we were refugees, but my parents always refused to accept money.

It was a very different experience to that of refugees arriving in Britain nowadays.

I feel very humble when I meet people who have struggled to come here as refugees. They are no different in many ways to my family. Like us back then, they too want to make a new home. And they too want to live here and to contribute to life in this country. ∎

Hassan

Iraq

I AM NEARLY 18. I have been in Oxford since June 2002. I come from a village near Mosul in northern Iraq. I am a Kurd. My family are still there. I left partly because I knew I would have to do military service when I was 18. I had also been picked up for buying Kurdish books in the market – this is forbidden. I was beaten and in hospital for 45 days. I got better but it was very expensive for my family.

Now I am learning English. I really like football. I used to be captain of the Mosul youth team. I played mid-field like David Beckham! My team was top of the league. Now I play in the park with my friends every day. I would like to be a footballer one day. ■

"I had been picked up for buying Kurdish books in the market. I was beaten and in hospital for 45 days."

Anne Tajfel

Germany

"We were given a booklet with some tips – about queuing, not shaking hands, but saying how do you do, and when someone asked 'How are you?' to answer, 'Very well, thank you,' even if you felt really bad."

I WAS ONCE a German Jewish refugee and I have been a British citizen for over 60 years. England is my home and I would not want to live anywhere else.

My early childhood was very happy. We lived near Hamburg in a thatched roofed house with a very large garden. My father was a prosperous businessman and a keen amateur violinist, and my mother was a painter who exhibited regularly. I was the middle of three daughters. We were liberal non-practising Jews. Before 1933 I hadn't been conscious of being Jewish. But then my uncle, a neuroscientist at Berlin University, was summarily dismissed in the middle of his experiments and left to take up an appointment at Cambridge University. He later helped us to get out.

My little life gradually changed. My best friend was no longer allowed to speak to me and neighbour's children no longer came to play in our garden. In my local primary school the children were assembled to sing the fascist anthem, arms outstretched in the 'Heil Hitler' salute. Then I was taken in by a Rudolf Steiner school who were anti Nazi. I remember not being allowed on stage for a school play and was given the part of an echo behind the curtain. And during a school outing I was not permitted to stay in a youth hostel with the other children.

In 1936 my father's firm was taken away from him. The Gestapo came to our house but we had friends who used to warn us in advance so that when they got there they only found the cook. We were still able to keep our loyal non-Jewish cook and gardener as they were over 60 years old. For a time I went to a Jewish school. I had to travel to Hamburg by train on my own everyday and learn to be inconspicuous. I never wore red. After the Gestapo took away one of the teachers I stayed at home.

I was somewhat lonely but I had my dolls to play with, read books from my parents' library, wrote my diary and went for long walks with my father. Restrictions tightened and now mother was only allowed to exhibit at a Jewish cultural centre. Father had to choose new Jewish musicians only for his chamber music evenings. Only Jewish doctors were allowed to treat us and holidays in Germany were no longer an option because hotels excluded Jews. A few of mother's artist colleagues did still visit but our social life grew ever smaller.

Meanwhile we were hearing stories. We all knew about Dachau, which was one of the first camps the Nazis set up, not just for Jews but for anti-fascists, gypsies and homosexuals as well. One of my grandparents rang from Berlin to say goodbye before committing suicide. He could not get a visa to leave.

Mother went to the city regularly to try to get emigration visas for us. But Britain did not give refugee status to Jews and as economic immigrants one had to bring money over and Germany would not release ours. Then came Kristallnacht and it became very urgent that we left. Luckily, my uncle had asked the headmistress of the Perse Girl's school in Cambridge to arrange for us girls to be enrolled at the school, so mother was able to obtain a visiting visa to accompany us. We had to leave father behind and of course everything else.

On 31st December 1938 we left very quietly without saying goodbye to anyone, each taking a large suitcase. I was allowed my violin, and took the plane to London where my uncle met us at Croydon airport. I was now a happy refugee in Cambridge. I felt free and safe. We moved into a small flat above a newspaper shop and Mother bought a few second-hand pieces at the Corn Exchange. She slept and painted in the living room where we also ate. It was hard for her, but I never heard her complain. We were given a booklet with some tips – about queuing, not shaking hands, but saying how do you do, and when someone asked 'How are you?' to answer 'Very well, thank you,' even if you felt really bad. Father had managed to get out somehow, with a suitcase and his violin and we were very glad when

war started in 1939 so that the parents could not be sent back. He was interned on the Isle of Man for the duration. We were classified 'Friendly Aliens' and had to take our Alien's Registration book with photo and fingerprints with us. We had to observe curfew and report to the police if we left for more than 24 hours. But it was war and our immediate family was intact. Cambridge was brilliant. All you needed was a second-hand bicycle and a library ticket. I went to school, learned English and made friends. A refugee committee sorted out problems and there was a club for older people to meet and talk in their native language without being conspicuous.

After I passed my matriculation I decided that I did not want to be a refugee any longer and joined the ATS (Auxilliary Territorial Service). I wanted to be part of the war effort and I wanted to belong. We were sent to an Ordnance depot in Shropshire. I lived in a Nissan hut with 14 young women and at first I could not always understand their jokes. When I got the hang of the English sense of humour and started dreaming in English I felt I truly belonged. After a stint as cook I progressed to the statistics office and ended up in the education corps. Every soldier had the right to one day's education a week and could choose among many courses. I taught German, history of opera, and I ran literacy classes and current affairs discussion groups. I met some very interesting people and formed lasting friendships. It was a hopeful time and social change was in the air. We discussed endlessly the possibilities of a social security system, the establishment of the National Health Service and education reforms. It was the first time in my life that I was able to vote.

After the war in 1946 I was demobilised, became a British citizen and was given an ex-service grant to study at Edinburgh University. I used to go to the public baths once a week with my soap and towel as my lodging only had gaslight and no bath. I wanted to be a teacher. My parents had also been naturalised, and settled in London to rebuild their lives together. They later bought a house in Highgate which had a lovely garden and they lived there for the rest of their lives.

It was while on vacation that I met my future husband Henri, and from that day on his life became very much my own. He was a Polish Jew, studying at the Sorbonne in Paris. When war broke out he joined the French army and from 1940 was a prisoner of war in Germany for five years. All his family perished in concentration camps. He became a French citizen and took a job as director of a French relief organisation looking after Jewish adolescent war orphans and camp survivors. Before we married in 1948 I told him that I wanted to live in Britain and bring up my children there.

But first we moved to occupied West Germany, where he worked for the International Refugee Organisation (United Nations) in a large Rehabilitation centre as Vocational Training Officer for displaced and disabled refugees. They were to be absorbed into the German economy or other countries. We lived in the British Zone in Osnabruck. I felt uncomfortable but nevertheless sorry for the people. Our first son was born during that period. I had become expert at packing and moving, but I was relieved when my husband got a working permit and we returned to Britain. Since it was hard to find accommodation in London, especially with a young child, I took a job as a cook/housekeeper, which had a rent-free flat in the semi basement, and my husband worked as a shipping clerk. He studied in the evenings at Birkbeck College, London University, as a part-time student and got a First in Psychology.

His first academic post was at Durham University, where our second son was born. Then he was appointed University Lecturer and Fellow of Linacre College at Oxford, where his academic career took off. For the first time we had a house of our own, the children went to school and we lived a normal life. In 1967 he became Professor of Social Psychology at Bristol University which was a fruitful time for him. He had of course become a British citizen but felt very European, so we enjoyed out holidays abroad. He was also visiting professor at universities in France, Holland, Italy, Israel, Canada and the US, and I sometimes joking referred to myself as a camp follower! In 1982 he was diagnosed with cancer. He wanted to die in Oxford. It was our last move together. Before we married he had said to me "If you want to marry a nine to five man, don't marry me: but with me you will never be bored." And I wasn't.

Afterwards I had intended to live in London near Hampstead Heath near where my parents had lived. But my two sons were still here then, so I stayed on. I have got used to Oxford again over the years; it can grow on you. The town is more multicultural, which suits me and there is even a little European coffee culture in some areas. The Town and Gown aspect no longer bothers me, and I enjoy the company of my young friends. Books, music and the lovely architecture keep me happy. And it's near London! As I am in my eighties now, I guess Oxford is a good place for the rest of my life. ∎

Jean Louis Ntadi
Congo Brazzaville

"The police came at six in the morning and told me to pack my bags. I was worried because I knew that people were taken away to be killed in this manner."

MY NAME IS Jean Louis Ntadi. I have a wife and six children. I am a playwright and poet from Congo Brazzaville. My play *Chef de l'Etat* (*The Chief of State*) was performed in a main theatre in Brazzaville. The Government thought the play was about them. The police came at six in the morning and told me to pack my bags. I was worried because I knew that people were taken away to be killed in this manner. I thought of trying to refuse to go but in the end went with them. I spent three days in a police station being interviewed and then 14 months in prison. I was tortured. I had no trial, nothing.

Then one day I was taken out of the prison and told to take a taxi home. I went into hiding, but I was still afraid of more night visits from the police so in the end I decided to leave my country. I wanted a visa to a francophone country as I don't speak English but in the end I got one for the UK.

I was not to know that my experience here was to be a different kind of torture.

At the airport I asked for asylum. This was in February 2004. But my asylum case was refused and I was sent to Oakington detention centre. Since then I have been through five detention centres, including Yarlswood and Belmarsh prisons and Campsfield House near Oxford. I had a hernia and was supposed to have an operation but instead I was moved to a new place. I was interviewed and humiliated and beaten up. On 26 May 2005 I was given bail and came out of Campsfield.

All this time I have been writing. I wrote *L'Acte de Naissance* (*The Act of Birth*) during my detention at Campsfield. I have been adopted by International PEN. My play *Cries of the Cricket* was performed on the London Eye and at the National Theatre in June 2005, as part of a celebration of African culture before the G8 Summit. Last November my play *Le Chef de l'Etat* won the Norwegian Playwrights' Solidarity Prize. And in December, some of the poems I wrote in detention were performed here in Oxford at the Burton Taylor Theatre.

But it has been harder here than in the Congo. I still have no news of my wife and children; I worry about them every day. And although I am now learning English, it is hard to communicate. My plays are my communication now; but I am still waiting for them to be translated and performed. ∎

Helen

Uganda

I WOULD LIKE to tell you about the difference between here and my home country, Uganda. Back home we never used to sit behind locked doors. Doors were always open. Here you eat, sleep and live behind locked doors.

In Uganda we are more friendly than you are here. People are laughing all the time. It is normal to cook extra food and invite people to eat in your house every day.

The strangest thing, however, was the snow! One day snow came and I wouldn't go out. 'What is this strange thing falling from the sky?' I said to my children. I couldn't think what to do.

Food too was very different. I was used to fresh fruit and vegetables from the land and fruit from the trees in my garden. It took me some time to find the Indian shop where I could buy okra and beans. You can buy sweet potato and cassava but they are very expensive.

Back home I had no cooker, no electricity, no running water. I cooked on a wood fire and would often walk a mile to fetch water, sometimes with a baby on my back. In Uganda women are all very strong – we have to do a lot of physical work. Here men change nappies, wash cups and plates. In Uganda you would go and dig in the field all day with your man and he would come back and sit and relax and you would clean the house, make food, look after the children; all the time the man would just be waiting to be served. I think that is one really good thing about this country – the men help more. At home the women do everything, the men only dig.

When I came here 15 years ago I came alone with two of my seven children. I had to run and leave my children behind. It was very hard. I had nine children, but two died in Uganda. Now all my children have come here, though my son David, who is an artist, has gone back to Uganda to build a school.

I came to Oxford because I knew someone here. I found the language very difficult. I was already old when I came and it was hard to learn a new language, new ways. I have never really managed to learn it so I could never get a job.

I went back to Uganda last July. There is still trouble in Gulu where I come from. I flew to Entebbe airport and stayed with friends in Kampala until we heard news that the road was clear. Then we had to travel the four hours in a convoy so that we were safe. It was sad to see the state of my country – the children begging. I cried for two days when I went back. There was nothing left for me there. My home had been burned, my land taken. Where would I go if I went back now?

My heart worries about my country though I know that my worries do not help. They just make me sick. But I also know that my country is a beautiful one. I pray every day that God will bless my country and it will become better. ∎

"In Uganda we are more friendly than you are here. People are laughing all the time. It is normal to cook extra food and invite people to eat in your house every day."

Bakhtiar

Iraq

"I feel I was born in a lorry in this country! But I have made many friends; there are about 40 young Kurdish people here from Iran, Iraq and Turkey, and we all share the same language and culture."

MY NAME IS Bakhtiar. I am 16. I am from Kirkuk, in Iraq. I am Kurdish. I have three small sisters and three small brothers. My family has no phone so I have no news of them.

I have been here six months. I left because I was in a car accident and an important policeman was hurt, and I knew I would be arrested and it would go very badly with me because I am Kurdish. So my family sent me out via Turkey and then I came to Oxford in a lorry. I had no idea where I was going or which country I would end up in. It took a long time to get here.

I feel I was born in a lorry in this country! But I have made many friends; there are about 40 young Kurdish people here from Iran, Iraq and Turkey, and we all share the same language and culture.

In my country there are many problems between Arabs and Kurds. Although now it is possible to learn Kurdish in school, I don't think otherwise the situation is improving much, from what I can see on the television.

I went to school and learned how to write Arabic. My dad taught me to read and write in Kurdish. I enjoyed taking the photographs and think they came out very well.

I don't know what will happen to me – I would like to be a doctor to help people. But first I need to learn English! ■

Albert
Ghana

I AM 16. I come from Ghana. I have been here in Oxford for three weeks. I had never left my village before. It is near the border with Côte d'Ivoire and one day bad people came from there and attacked us. I was living with my father. I don't know where he is now. I had to leave. I escaped with some friends and came to England. But I lost my friends in London. Most of the time I am just alone in the house. ∎

"I was living with my father. I don't know where he is now. I had to leave. I escaped with some friends and came to England. But I lost my friends in London."

Professor Leszek Kolakowski

Poland

"There are many things about Britain that I found strange when I first came here in the summer of 1970 – for example, you had separate taps for hot and cold water."

I WAS BORN in Poland in 1927 and because of the German occupation of Poland did not attend school, but had private lessons. I studied philosophy at Lodz University and gained my doctorate from Warsaw University in 1953. I was working as professor of philosophy at the university but becoming increasingly disillusioned with the Communist Government. They were also not fond of me. I made a number of scandals, which the Government considered dangerous – I was seen as an enemy of Communism. In 1968, I was dismissed from my job and expelled from the university, along with five other professors.

There was a lot of publicity about this. The security police watched my house day and night with the aim of intimidating me. Along with a number of other people, I was not allowed to publish. This meant it was impossible to work.

I was invited to teach at McGill University in Canada, but it was not easy to leave. After several months I succeeded in getting a passport for myself and my wife and daughter, and we flew to Canada. I taught in French because my English was not so good at that point. I spent 1968 and 1969 there and then went to the University of Berkeley, California. But I didn't want to stay in the US – I thought the schools were better here for my daughter. And 1968 was a bad year for education in America with all sorts of so-called revolutions, with Berkeley the centre of the trouble.

Then people here at All Souls College suggested I should apply and I was elected a Fellow. I am still an emeritus member of the College.

There are many things about Britain that I found strange when I first came here in the summer of 1970 – for example, you had separate taps for hot and cold water. And coffee espresso machines did not exist – though they do now!

I had very friendly feelings towards the British people – I found them very reliable and trustworthy. But I noticed that when I met people with whom it was really easy to communicate they were always partly foreign – Irish or Jewish.

I travelled a lot during the following years, also teaching at the University of Chicago and at Yale. I kept my Polish passport but had to validate it every year. At a certain moment the authorities refused to validate it – so I applied for British citizenship. After the collapse of Communism in Poland I was given back my Polish passport. I went back to Poland at the end of 1988 for the first time in 20 years. It was nearing the end of the regime – I was interrogated by the political police; they accused me of breaking some rules, but it was not serious and there were no consequences.

Even after so many years I don't really have the feeling of belonging here in Britain. Although I have never lived in France for more than six months, somehow I feel more at home in Paris than I do here. My daughter has lived in Paris for many years. As far as my nationality is concerned, I still feel Polish. In English, nationality and citizenship are the same meaning; in other languages it is more possible to separate the two. So I am a citizen of Britain now but I am also Polish.

My wife has been with me all the time – she has similar feelings. She likes England, but it is a foreign country. I thought about going back to Poland, but so many things would have to be arranged – I prefer to stay here now. ∎

Grace
Uganda

"I believe in the saying: 'You make your home where God leads you to, wherever that may be.' An individual well equipped with knowledge of where they are, who they are and where they are from has the best of both worlds."

MY NAME IS Grace Rwotlakica. By the age of six I had already been displaced and had moved homes several times in my life, due to civil war in my country, Uganda.

I came to England with my mother and my siblings in the week I turned seven. I remember it was very hot when we left, but we arrived in England when it was icy cold, frosty and thickly foggy. Luckily my grandfather, uncle and several other family friends and a member of our church were there at Gatwick airport, waiting for us with warm winter coats and thermos flasks of hot tea.

Although my mother and the older people in our home had heard over the radio that my father had been shot dead the previous April, it wasn't until January the following year, a few days before our flight to Britain, that I remember my older sister reading a newspaper and crying bitterly. Only then did I find out. At that very early age I realised how cruel death can be, for it had separated me from a father I loved so dearly.

The hardest thing about moving home was not leaving toys or material things behind. We were brought up with the knowledge that family and our Christian faith were our most precious belonging. 'If you must take nothing else, you take God; the rest doesn't really matter,' I remember being told.

I found school in England very different from Uganda – for example, I was really surprised to have cooking lessons at school. I had been able to cook from the age of five from watching my mother and sisters. My teacher soon realised this and used to ask me to cook Ugandan recipes. She even entered me for the Junior Master Chefs competition at the age of 12. That was great.

I remember another time at school, not so positive, when we were asked to write down our earliest memories.

Having shared so many happy memories about being a child in Uganda, I decided to write about what I had seen during the civil war. My teacher read it and told me that I was 'making it up'. That I had 'a vivid imagination'.

I didn't sleep for weeks, and after that I ended up telling myself these experiences were just bad dreams. It was not until many years later that my mother revealed to me that the events had actually happened just as I recalled them.

I still think of Uganda as home, though I have spent more of my life here in the UK than I did there. I have adapted to the English culture quite well. I have never been back to Uganda.

I believe in the saying: 'You make your home where God leads you to, wherever that may be.' An individual well equipped with knowledge of where they are, who they are and where they are from has the best of both worlds; they can enrich their lives with the wisdom from both places.

I'm blessed to have two homes: Uganda and Oxford. ∎

Shahrzad

Iran

"One day six months later I told my mother I was going out for some fresh air. I wish I had never gone out that day."

WHEN THE ISLAMIC revolution happened I was 14. I lived with my family in a town about the size of Oxford called Amol, near the Caspian Sea. I have one brother and two sisters and we had a happy life. I had many friends and I loved cycling. I was quite entrepreneurial even then. I dreamed of a very special bike that cost £500. My father gave me £100 and to raise the rest of the money I bought socks and hats from people who had been to the market in Tehran and sold them in school. I had a special kiosk and I ran my business in the afternoon after school had finished. It took me two years but one day I was able to buy my dream bicycle!

The first I knew of the revolution was seeing lots of police cars down the narrow alleyway beside my school. On the wall someone had written 'Down with the Shah!' The police had closed the area around the school in order to find out who wrote those words.

Three or four months later we were starting to hear about Ayatollah Khomeini. I was not at all religious and had friends who were Muslims, Christians and Jews. It was at that time I found out my family was Shi'a Muslim and we were no longer supposed to visit friends from other religions.

Then my school closed completely. The whole country was on strike against the Shah. There were many demonstrations but I stayed at home. We listened to the news. Khomeini arrived in Iran exactly one week and 28 years ago today.

After six months the school opened again and there were normal lessons again. But there was a different atmosphere. We heard about all the bad things the Shah had done. People seemed to get more aggressive. It made me feel that I did not like any of them and at the age of 16 I became a socialist. There was a group of boys and girls who got together and talked about politics, something we had not been able to do under the Shah. I sold socialist newspapers in the street.

But then in my last year at school everything was turned upside down. The police started breaking down people's doors and catching everyone who belonged to a group. It became very scary. I remember the day my mother said that I should leave and go and stay in a village in the mountains where we had a summer house. I didn't want to leave my studies but I knew town was a dangerous place to be and I would be safer out of the city.

For two years I worked in my uncle's restaurant in the village. My parents came to visit me but I was not allowed to go home. I spent time with my cousin, who at 22 was older than me but became my friend and we had many long discussions.

Then one night they came for my cousin. He was arrested and taken away. My father decided it was no longer safe for me to stay in the village and took me to Tehran, where my sister lived with her husband. There was nothing to do, just eat and sleep, eat and sleep. I couldn't get out because I had no ID if anyone stopped me.

After six months my sister went back to Amol and I went on to a different town even further from home where my father had a good friend. I stayed there another six months until the friend told my father that the neighbours were asking questions and it was no longer safe for me to stay.

My father came and picked me up and took me home. On the way into Amol police were searching cars and I had to put my head down until we drove into the courtyard of my home. No-one except my family knew I was back.

I stayed in my house for a couple of months. Once again, I was not allowed to go out and had nothing to do. This was very hard for me as a young man. But there were revolutionary police patrolling the streets.

Then we heard that my cousin had been executed. Once again I hid in the car and my family took me back to the village in the mountains.

We arrived just in time for the big party that my uncle and father held each year to celebrate the planting of their crops. There were about 100 people and it was wonderful to be out in a crowd

again. I fell in love with a girl from Amol. It was amazing!

When she went back home a week later I told my family I was going to Amol as well. I had had enough of hiding. I rode my bicycle to her house every evening but didn't dare go inside. I stood there for half an hour hoping she would come out. She didn't.

However, nothing happened to me either and I decided to go back to school. We had a family member who was a revolutionary guard and he wrote a letter for me, which helped me get back into school, though I was older than the other students and everyone wondered where I had been for the past three years.

One day, six months later, I told my mother I was going out for some fresh air. I wish I had never gone out that day. It was a Friday, the time when people were supposed to be at prayer, and my mother didn't want me to go. A private car stopped in front of me and started reversing. A man got out and asked me to get in the car. I said: 'We are having guests at home and I have to get some meat and take it back for my mother.'

They took me to a place I shouldn't have been. I had to sit close to a wall and was not allowed to move. I was not allowed to go to the toilet. I was put in a cell with six other people. One man told me he had been there for three years and thought he was going to be executed.

It took me a year to get out. I don't want to tell you what happened to me in that time. My family managed it through our connection with the same revolutionary guard who had helped me get back into school.

I was still in love with the girl I had met in the mountains but her family did not want to know me because I had been in prison.

I finished school and was sent to do military service. I learned a lot. After three month's training I was sent to another military academy in Rasht. I remember one day on the parade ground the officer said that anyone who had been in prison should step out of line. One person stepped out. I couldn't decide what to do – if I stepped out, what would happen to me? If I didn't and they knew I had been in prison, what would happen? I was sweating. In the end I decided not to step out. It was the right decision.

During the three months I spent there I studied and was accepted at the university in Tehran. I still had 18 months military service which I would have to complete after finishing university but at that point the war with Iraq had started so I was happy to get out.

I went to university for two years and studied accountancy. I had a fantastic time. I started a business selling goldfish for the four weeks of Persian New Year and made quite a lot of money. One day I heard a voice and looked up and it was the girl I had fallen in love with! We went out for a while but it didn't work out.

I continued my business after I went back to do my military service, as I was free in the afternoons. By then I had a flat in Rasht. I also bought a video camera and started making wedding films.

After my military service I moved to Tehran. It was 1993 and there was a demonstration against the regime, I think because people wanted water or food. I filmed the demonstration but was spotted by the revolutionary guard. I dropped my camera and unfortunately it also contained my business card with my address. They destroyed everything in my flat. I had to hide for six months and decided it was time to leave the country.

I paid $3,000 to get out of Iran via Turkey. It was winter and very cold. I had only a small bag with me. I went on foot and by road and eventually ended up in Holland where I was told to go to a police station and ask for asylum.

In Holland I spent six months in one asylum centre and another year in a different one. I was well treated and people were friendly. There were people from Somalia, former Yugoslavia, Iran, Iraq, and Angola. I still have a picture of one group of us.

I learned English and Dutch and Serbo-Croat. After 18 months I was able to move around, and had some pocket money. But it was a depressing life and there was no news of what would happen to me next.

Then one day an Iranian friend of mine went to the shower. When he didn't come back for a long time, I went to find him. He had left the water running and killed himself.

After that I decided I had to move on. I contacted the man who had originally brought me to Holland and asked him if he could get me to Canada. He could – for a price. I called my father and he sold his car to get me the money. I was given a false passport and took a train to France and then to England where I ended up in Manchester. From there I bought a ticket to Canada. But when I got there they said I didn't have enough money or any contacts and put me straight on a plane back to Manchester.

They must also have told the British authorities that there was something wrong with my passport because I was detained at 4 am and given the choice of being sent back to Iran or applying for political asylum. It was not much of a choice. I spent a week in a detention centre at the airport and they told me I was going to Oxfordshire. Where was that? I wondered.

I was put in a car. I was very afraid they were going to deport me. I arrived at Campsfield House, a detention centre for asylum seekers near Oxford, where I was to stay for 9 months and 11 days.

After a few months, one of the Campsfield visitors who spoke Persian tracked me down. She was called Shahin. I was crying. I hadn't spoken Persian for a long time. She found a solicitor who located my file in Holland. It took two attempts to get me out on bail.

After I got out, I stayed with Shahin for six months. During that time I had to sign in at the police station every week. Then I found a room in Oxford and went to college to learn English. I got a job in a travel agency after 1998, when I had temporary permission to stay and permission to work. In 2002, I was granted full refugee status and in 2005 I became a British citizen and got my passport.

I am now a postmaster in an Oxford Post Office and sign passport forms for other people applying for citizenship. I also continue to make films, sometimes travelling around Europe to do so. I have not yet been back to Iran. Oxford is my home now – when I am travelling and I come back into British airspace, it feels like coming home. ∎

Amina

Rwanda

"People were not very friendly at first. But once they get to know you they are more friendly. White people in Africa are not treated like this: people will be friendly, they will invite you in."

MY NAME IS Amina. I am aged 16, from Rwanda. I am studying healthcare at college in Oxford. When I came here I didn't speak any English – but I learned fast! When we first moved to the house in the Abingdon Road we would go to the pool and we would be the only black people. Even walking down the street we would feel that people stared at these two black girls as if to say: 'What are you doing here?' We would feel them looking from behind their net curtains. It wasn't bad, but you just felt that you stood out. People were not very friendly at first. But once they get to know you they are more friendly. White people in Africa are not treated like this: people will be friendly, they will invite you in. It is part of our culture. Perhaps because we have more time... or because it is warm. When I first came here I was so cold. I remember someone saying it was minus four degrees. I couldn't imagine this. In Africa it is never cold.

I didn't like all the old buildings in Oxford either. They are so old! I like new buildings, with shopping centres and cinemas. What is the point of all these old buildings? At home, our culture is not preserved in buildings but by people – they hand down the stories to their children and their children's children.

In Africa, time is different too. When I first came here they made me appointments with the doctor, the social worker etc. The appointment would be at three and I didn't realise I had to turn up exactly at three. At home if you have an appointment at three you might turn up at four and they would still see you - they would not consider that you were late. But here time is different. I found that hard at first.

When I wear the scarf over my head, especially when it covers most of my face, I feel hidden, as though I am hiding, private. But I also feel protected. When I wear Western clothes I feel freer. I have a different identity in these British clothes. I would never wear these party clothes at home! Never! People would think you are a prostitute or something. But here in my party clothes I feel ready to party!

In the scarf (called a *bui bui*) I feel secure; people don't notice you, or if they do they don't know who you are because they can't see you! It was great when I was little, because in school if you were naughty, and everyone was wearing this, we would run away and the teacher couldn't tell you off because they didn't know who you were!

Then when I was six my family, which had been Muslim, became Christian and we didn't wear the *bui bui* any more. I don't know why they changed; for me, it meant wearing different clothes and learning the Bible instead of the Qur'an. Otherwise it didn't make much difference; but now I am a Christian and I go to church here in Oxford. ∎

Annelie Rookwood

Germany

I WAS BORN in Dachau in 1928 before it became a concentration camp. Given that my parents were living in Berlin this was strange, but I did not hear the full story until 1970. I remained an only child. Our surname was Sluzewski from earlier generations of refugees.

My father was a lawyer in private practice. As the Nazi scene developed and they came to power in 1933, he realised very quickly that he had to get his family out fast. He set up an office in London in 1934 but we did not leave as a family until January 1937. At that point we came to Southampton, complete with all our goods, including the family car. We drove into London in style - not at all the usual image of a refugee family!

During those last German years my parents protected me very carefully. We were now living in Dahlem, a suburb of Berlin. My memories of those last years are slim. It was all little things, like losing the right to live in the whole of our house after 1934 - we were shunted upstairs and lost a lot of space. I was bullied at school and very isolated. After Kristallnacht in 1938, Jewish children were removed from schools, no longer allowed to use parks, swimming pools or other public places. My grandparents were still in Germany at that point and it was a major struggle to get permits both to leave Germany and to enter Britain. I still have a passport of my grandmother's with a big 'J' stamped on the cover. They left in 1939.

When we reached London my father had already got a furnished flat for us in Kensington. My mother, ever resourceful, found me a little private school nearby so that I could start to learn English.

My father, a very good violinist, had always played in a string quartet and in the end all four players and their families were evacuated to England. The music went on and we all remained close friends. A big fat book exists of all the programmes played from 1924 until 1970.

In June 1938 we moved into our own house in Hampstead Garden Suburb, close to acres of heathland to roam in. It was a strange choice; we were hidden in a little close and my mother was desperately lonely. She was not used to being alone all day and she had very little English. Her neighbours took very little notice of her except to ask her to tea once.

The War was her salvation - people mixed more and everybody faced the same dangers. My three grandparents came to live with us. My father had to finance us all, despite work drying up for him.

By June 1940 my father, along with most German and Austrian male refugees, was interned on the Isle of Man. He was fine there and had good company. But we had little contact with him.

When war broke out I was on holiday in Devon. I made friends with a little girl there and my mother asked her parents to take me back to Evesham with them, not wanting to take a child back to London. I remember going off in the car with them and my mother coming later and bringing my clothes. I stayed there for two terms. In a sense I was a refugee again - living on a farm with the family plus two scruffy boys who were evacuees from Birmingham. However, I missed home badly and hated my little private school.

By Easter 1940 I was back home again. It seemed safe. But then the Blitz broke out over our heads and my mum, a friend of hers and her daughter who was the same age as me were evacuated to Surrey. I was at a little boarding school. The two mothers got rooms in a farm nearby.

The two mothers decided to move up to Keswick as it seemed there was a real chance of Hitler invading. We went to school there and had a wonderful time. It was a bitterly cold winter and Keswick lake froze over and we could skate on it.

By summer 1943 we moved back to London - it seemed peaceful but of course was not. On the journey home I was in charge of a bucket of farm eggs in a jelly-like preserve. Eggs were scarce - one per person per week - but farmers still had spare.

I went to St Paul's Girls School. I had to travel

across London and the bombs were still dropping, so it was scary. I remember the doodlebugs when I was writing my school certificate. My father swore I only passed Latin because the exams were suspended because of the bombing.

In 1947 I left St Paul's and went to Edinburgh University to study geography. I lived at home in London with my parents until I married in 1954. I met my husband Ralph when we were both working for the London County Council. Ralph came from Canada; his mother's family had emigrated from Czechoslovakia in 1910 to Alberta.

We lived in London for the first two years of our marriage and there was lots of discussion about a possible move to India, where Ralph and some colleagues had been asked to set up a town planning school. But it never happened and we spent four years in Canada before coming back to England. We were in Cambridge for four years, then we moved back to London, both of us working in planning. When Ralph retired we moved to Oxford and have been here since 1982.

It was not until 1970 when my father died that I discovered the truth about my parentage. He had a heart attack on holiday and left me as sole executor. I had worked in his office at one point for the best part of a year and so had some legal training. When I went through his stuff I remember my mother saying: 'If you find any personal things, please let me look at it rather than you.' I thought it was a bit odd at the time. The only thing I found was a file labelled 'birth and death certificates' and I didn't think much about it at the time. I put it away and forgot about it.

Six months later I decided to look at the file. It contained my grandparents' birth certificates but also a brown paper envelope with an official red seal marked: 'Annelie's birth certificate'. Inside was a piece of paper with details of my real mother's name and my birth certificate. I was with my birth mother for a very short time and then went to an orphanage. From the notes in the margin of the certificate it was clear that my biological father adopted me in 1929.

I didn't know what to do. I left it for a while. I had four children of my own by then. But I found it was getting between me and the woman I had always considered to be my mother. So I sat her down and told her I had found my birth certificate and asked her what she knew. She said: 'Nothing' – she may indeed have known very little herself, knowing my father.

I tried talking to some of my father's close friends but they all said they didn't know anything. It turned out that when I was a child everyone except me had known that I was adopted. My father's sister said she did not know anything either. A friend of mine who was a lawyer in Germany tried to track down the orphanage but it was no longer there and all pre-War documents had been lost. I am pretty sure that my father was indeed my biological father as my children look so much like him.

I think my mother must have died when I was young and certainly my father and my adoptive mother had been married for five years before they went to find me in the orphanage. But there was nothing else I could find out and it was a huge struggle coming to terms with this.

It made me think about my heritage but it was not until after Ralph's death that I found myself thinking about being Jewish and even talking with a slight German accent again – after all these years. Now I am beginning to meet other Jewish people, former refugees. In many ways, the wheel has come full circle. ∎

Arafa
Somalia

"I came with some other adults and they brought me to Oxford. They dropped me off and told me to wait for them. But they never came back. I waited and waited all day. I was so cold."

MY NAME IS Arafa. I am 17 and originally from Somalia. I only came to Oxford and to the UK three months ago, but I have spent the last 10 years in Mombasa, Kenya. My dad was killed when I was young and my mum brought me and my elder brother to Mombasa when I was seven. At that time I couldn't walk because there was something wrong with my leg and could only get around using my hands. She left me with a family who had one small baby. They arranged for me to have many operations and then I could walk at last. But my mum never came back. I grew up calling the parents in the other family 'Mummy' and 'Daddy' although in fact I wasn't treated as a daughter; I was really a house girl. They had two more children and I washed nappies, cooked, scrubbed floors. It was hard work. I wasn't able to go to school so I never learned to read and write in Swahili, my language.

Then last year my 'mummy' said it was time for me to get married. She took me to meet my future husband. He was an old man! I said I would never marry him and I cried and cried. Then my 'daddy', who was a businessman, said that if I wouldn't marry him I would be sent away. He put me on a bus to Nairobi and arranged a plane to the UK. I came with some other adults and they brought me to Oxford. We were going to go to the shops as I didn't have any warm clothes or anything and they dropped me off and told me to wait for them. But they never came back. I waited and waited all day. I was so cold. Then at last I heard someone talking Swahili on a mobile phone and I told them my story and asked them for help. They took me to Social Services, which was just closing, but they opened up for me and found me somewhere to stay. The next day they took me to the doctor and he gave me some medicine because I had been so cold waiting.

Now I am studying English and I am learning fast, as you see because you can talk to me in English. The teacher was also amazed because I found I could write with both my left and my right hand. I stay in the house a lot because I don't know many people. I would like to find my mother and brother. Maybe one day I would like to study the hotel business. ∎

Maqboull
Somalia

"Many people think foreign people come to bring problems to this country but not many strangers are problem-makers. Just as many bring benefits to the country."

MY NAME IS Maqboull. I am 20 years old. I was born in Kismayu, Somalia. I have been here for four years. I am studying business studies, science and horticulture at college. I am good at maths and maybe I would like to study accountancy. I like studying and helping people in any situation. My aim is to help poor people all over the world. Many people think foreign people come to bring problems to this country but not many strangers are problem-makers. Just as many bring benefits to the country.

I like to play football and I support Arsenal football club. I have played football in my country, but I wasn't as good as I am now because here I can play more and I have gained in confidence and experience and feel more in control of the ball. In Africa sports are more informal – you see people playing football on the beach, in the street. You can even play barefoot – I used to do this. Your feet are much harder when you don't wear shoes all the time.

Now I can pretend to play in many different styles - like Beckham, Zidane, Ronaldinho, Henry.

I can play as a mid-fielder, striker, right and left wing because I can use both legs when I play. I have made many friends, both British and foreign, through playing football. It is a good way of meeting people. It also helps you to get fit and that makes you feel positive about life and drives away any negative feelings. I would like to succeed in football but there is one thing that keeps me back. If you have any talent you do not know how to make it known and how to find an organisation to help you in organising that talent. I would like to find clubs that have competitions like professional clubs.

The difference between this country and Somalia is that this country is so cold. The weather is very different compared with the weather in my country. I miss my parents. I miss swimming and playing on the beach. I used to live near the beach.

I like this country because I feel I am free. Nobody can disturb me. If they do, the government will arrest them. So I am safe to go anywhere in this country or in other European countries. ∎

Orlando Trujillo-Bueno

Colombia

"A local Senator called me. He asked me to give up my campaign for human rights – he said he could get me a good grant for me to study. He said all this in a nice way – until I said no, of course."

I WAS BORN in a small town near a big city called Calli, in Colombia. I trained as a doctor in my country and practised as a GP for three years. I then moved into forensic medicine. I was involved in teaching at the University of Colombia, showing students how to do a *postmortem* and assess injuries.

After this, I got a new job in a hospital outside Calli. On my first day, I got a phone call. A man's voice told me that a wounded patient would shortly arrive in the hospital and warned me to do nothing to help him. A few minutes later a wounded patient was brought in. We drained the blood from his lung and sent him to another hospital to be treated. I then got another phone call telling me to do as I was told. But as a doctor I believe that you are a leader of the community and need to behave in an ethical way.

This was to prove an increasingly dangerous point of view, because Calli at the time was the centre of a drug cartel that had moved from Medellin. They were in league with all sorts of people in high places – the President at the time even thanked them for the lovely diamond they gave his wife!

I soon found out what it was like to be a doctor under those circumstances. When the cartel put pressure on a judge to release one of their men, the judges would throw the ball into the doctor's court. 'It depends on the forensic report', they would say. We were offered money, and if we didn't co-operate there were threats. Many doctors were killed, including colleagues of mine. One was shot at a traffic light. Before he died he asked me to look after his 75-year-old mum. I then got anonymous calls telling me not to see her.

Things got worse when one of my colleagues accepted money to write a dodgy report. It was refuted and came back to us for a second opinion. The colleague who had written the original report got upset and put a lot of pressure on us, but we would not write an untrue report. It was an unsettling situation. I was also involved in human rights activities, raising my voice against what I saw was wrong. We used to visit prisoners in army places to do reports on their state of health. I am sad to say that some had clearly been injured while they were detained. As a result, a member of the army intelligence became very friendly with me, keeping a constant eye on what I was doing. He used to come up to me in the car park and pretend to shoot me. He had a very weird sense of humour!

In all these activities I didn't really think about the consequences – we started support groups in the area for those who wanted to use democracy to change the system, and to minimise corruption. I joined a civic political party led by a very brave former priest. We set up a network of judges, journalists, doctors and academics. But in Colombia, if you are a doctor and you work for the government you are not allowed to take part in politics. A local Senator called me. He asked me to give up my campaign for human rights – he said he could get me a good grant for me to study. He said all this in a nice way – until I said no, of course.

After that the situation became completely unsafe. In 1990 I was forced to leave the country. A lot of things happened with my family after I left – they had to move house. An uncle who was a judge was killed.

I found it very hard being here in England. I didn't speak a word of English, and I just wanted to get back home. After a year I moved from London to Oxford and some friends arranged for me to stay with a family who only spoke English. I was very low at the time. But I decided I must learn English so I took my Spanish-English dictionary to Oxford Polytechnic (now Oxford Brookes University) and found someone to teach me. I was keen to start practising medicine again as soon as I could.

I was lucky to meet a friend from Chile who is a psychiatrist. He was working in a hospital in Milton Keynes and living in Oxford. I travelled with him each day and worked in his hospital – in this way I learned how an English hospital functions and continued to learn English. It was not easy; I still

find there are things I want to say that I can only say in Spanish.

From there I moved into further academic study. I applied to the Institute of Psychiatry in London to do a Masters degree in neuroscience. I got a grant from the Society for the Protection of Science and Learning which was set up during the Second World War for professionals who had to flee their country. I think Einstein was among their numbers! I remember I sent over 300 letters before I found a grant.

But I had enormous support when writing my thesis.

I then went on to take the General Medical Council's (GMC) exams that you need to become a doctor in the UK. I passed, but to my surprise they told me that I still could not practise because my medical school in Colombia was not recognised. I wrote and told them that I didn't accept this - my school was one of the best in the country and people came from Harvard to study there if their parents were Colombian.

In the end they told me I could apply to the Society of Apothecaries, a body which gives licences to doctors not licensed by the GMC. But they told me that I would need to go back to university and retake my final year as a medical student. I applied to university but found that I would have to pay £14,000-£15,000 in medical fees. Thanks to support from many quarters I had raised £5,000 in grants, but this amount was impossible. In the meantime, I was offered a job as a research assistant in Glasgow. I worked there for three years and started a PHD. In that time got exceptional leave to remain in this country. But I was still determined to become a doctor. I got a place at Glasgow Medical School, so I gave up my job and PhD to do the final year.

I did not realise it, but there was still one hurdle to get through - an examination at the Society of Apothecaries. This cost £750, and you had to pass a written exam, a viva and a clinical examination. I did not get through the first time - it had not been clear to me what I had to do. On the second attempt I met many people who were on their third or fourth attempt. You are only allowed five attempts. One man was crying because he was now so deeply in debt. I went into that exam in a challenging mood. A gynaecologist asked me what I had read in the papers about his subject and I said I hadn't been reading the papers lately because I had been focusing on the exam. He told me that medical students have to read! I failed the exam.

By this time I was in real financial trouble. I decided I would never be a doctor again. So I did a four-year course in acupuncture and two years of psychotherapy. I set up my own private practice in Scotland. But I kept in touch with the GMC because in my heart I had never really given up on being a doctor again.

Finally, in 2001, I got a letter to say that my medical school in Colombia was now recognised by the GMC. I had been out of practice for many years by this time so I had to take another exam. I was also busy by that time with the Centre for Forensic International Assistance that I had helped to set up at the University of Glasgow. It aimed to investigate human rights abuses in places like Kosovo, in a neutral and scientific way.

But in 2003 I decided to leave the Centre and came to Oxford. I joined the Refugee Doctors Professional group and got a job as a project co-ordinator on a mental health project. I then worked on a research project funded by the Home Office about communicating with next of kin about *postmortem* findings. I was really interested in becoming a psychiatrist. I am now working as a Senior House Officer in the Psychiatry department of an Oxford teaching hospital. It has taken me a long time, but I am almost there at last. ∎

Florence

Kenya

MY NAME IS Florence. I am 17 years old and studying to be a nurse at the same college as Amina and Fidelis. I am Kenyan, from Mombasa and I came here when I was 13, so I have been in England for four years now. I like Oxford and have made friends here.

I have a sister who is eight years old – though she has a much bigger frame than I do and will be bigger than me one day.

I like being in Oxford. I like my friends at college and I like walking and just sitting in the parks – even when it is cold!

I want to be a nurse because I like to help people and I like being with people. I would like to study nursing at university. ∎

"I want to be a nurse because I like to help people and I like being with people. I would like to study nursing at university."

Makonen Getu
Ethiopia

"Three months later I was on the road and I bumped into a military government leader whom I used to know. He grabbed me by the neck and asked me what I was doing."

WHAT AMAZES ME in my life is that I am still alive. I should have died as a child in Ethiopia, when I was tending cattle and living a poor life in a remote village. Or as an adult, or indeed at any point in my life. It is likely that I would not be here if I had not had the opportunity of going to school.

As a small child, I was sick all the time. My dad took me away from my mum at the age of three – that is a very long story. My dad and I lived in a very remote village and when my health improved, I started looking after cattle. At the age of eight, my dad decided to send me to school. At that time I didn't even know what school was! It was thanks to my uncle, who was the most progressive person in my family. He introduced the first retail shop in the village and was a business leader. He was the only one in the family who could read and write and one day he found me in his house looking at our equivalent of a *Book of Psalms* with great interest, though I couldn't understand anything. I think it was he who encouraged my dad to send me to school.

My school was an hour's walk from home. I remember two scary things on those journeys, which I sometimes shared with my uncle's son, who was older than me but was sent to school at the same time. The first was the fierce dogs, which were there to guard the village and did just that, barking and chasing me. The second was the boys from other villages who would tease and shout at me, especially when I was on my own. At the first school I went to I soon learned all the priest could teach me, and was teaching other pupils. We used to go to the toilet in the bush and one day I just excused myself and never went back. I told my uncle that I needed to go to another school and he took me there. The head teacher said: 'You can start tomorrow morning. But you must be here by 8 am.' I had no idea of time and slept with everyone else in the bushes by the village. That night I didn't sleep at all and got to school so early that even the birds had not woken up.

I did an eight-year programme in five years. The high school I went to was three days' walk from my village so I used to live with other students. I became politically engaged – there was so much injustice in a country where 90 per cent of people were so poor they had no land. I was very active in the school, leading different associations and becoming chief editor of the school magazine. In those days under Haile Selassie, who ruled as an absolute monarch, anything that was written, even for a school magazine, had to go to the Ministry of Information for checking. I remember writing an article, a very good article, called 'Only Today'. It was about rats and cats, comparing the peasants to the rats and those who exploited them to the cats. It never got published.

In our school we had Swedish teachers who came as volunteers. In the holidays I used to work on a Swedish project. In 1971 I finished high school and went to Addis Ababa University. Students were very active there and at one stage it was closed down.

Although I was offered scholarships elsewhere, I decided to go to Sweden. I went as a tourist and had no money. I got work as a babysitter and as a cleaner and started studying. I needed level 4 Swedish if I was to go to university and was told it usually took two years. But I was in a hurry and did it in six months. There were three different government-funded language centres so I went to one in the morning, one in the afternoon and one in the evening. But I still couldn't speak well and it wasn't until I went to spend Christmas with a family that I suddenly started speaking! I managed to pass the exam after six months and then went to university. It was tough because I found it hard to understand the lectures. But luckily many of the documents were in English and I could also take the exams in English. So I managed to get my degree in two and a half years while also working for my living in a computer department.

After that I got a scholarship and studied

for my PhD. I became a Swedish citizen. I was heavily involved in politics. I was the leader of the Ethiopian student movement in Sweden. It was a huge movement. At that time student movements in Iran and Ethiopia were the largest in the world. While we were agitating against the Emperor, in Iran they were against the Shah.

In 1974, low-ranking officers in Ethiopia overthrew the monarchy. They had embraced our political line on land reform, democracy and socialism. We gave them critical support. I was part of the All Ethiopian Socialist Movement, which was very influential at the time.

In 1977 our organisation reached a point where the military government felt threatened. At the May Day celebrations people came out in force supporting us and the military reacted by threatening and imprisoning our members. In July we went underground. Within six months the military had captured and killed many of us. It was a time known as the White and Red Terror.

The organisation decided to bring in some people from outside the country to replace them. I was one of these. I told my friends and even my girlfriend in Sweden that I was going to Canada to do research. My organisation told me that someone would meet me at the airport but when I got there no-one was there. It was horrible. I decided to take a taxi but I didn't even have any Ethiopian money and it was illegal at the time to have dollars. I had no passport either, as they had taken it at the airport – this was common practice at the time. And I had no Ethiopian ID card so no hotel would take me. I decided to visit a friend of a friend. He wasn't in and the guard told me to wait outside the gate. When he came, he was very disappointed to see me. He already had my friend hiding in his house and it put him in danger. But he allowed me to stay for a week on condition I did not move anywhere.

After that my organisation gave me a gun (which I never used), a place to stay and 100 Ethiopian birr a month (about £45) and a list of contacts. I travelled around a lot. Three months later I was on the road and I bumped into a military government leader whom I used to know. He grabbed me by the neck and asked me what I was doing. You become very creative in these circumstances. You never run out of ideas about how to keep alive. I told him I had left the student movement and was doing research. I was surprised how calm I was. He became very friendly.

The moment he left, the fear swallowed me. I wished the earth could have swallowed me up. For the following nine months I never slept in the same place for two consecutive nights. I heard from our people in the State House that he had reported that I was in the country. One night I had arranged to meet one of my closest friends. He never turned up. I decided it was not safe to stay there and spent the night in a prostitute's house. It was so dirty I didn't want to take off my clothes. It was also risky. I knew the militias came to such houses. It was that night that I decided to leave the country. It was two in the morning and I knelt down and said: 'God, if you save my life I will believe in you.' This was the desperate state that I, a Marxist, who had believed that religion was the opium of the people, had come to.

When after many adventures I finally managed to leave the country I went back to Sweden. I gave up politics, started studying again and teaching.

I didn't keep my promise to God. But one day one of my students gave me a copy of the New Testament. It reminded me of that promise. Two months later I met my wife at a jazz club. She comes from a Christian background in Finland. I was introduced to her father, who is a very well-read man. He said: 'No-one should tell Makonen to believe in God. He should find the way himself.' And in 1983 I became a Christian. I kept my promise.

Since then my path has taken me to Lesotho and Zambia, working for the United Nations and for World Vision and now Opportunity International, which is a micro-financing organisation. In 2000, my family and I came to Oxford where we have lived ever since. ■

Mohamed

Iran

MY NAME IS Mohamed. I am 18. I am Kurdish, from Iranian Kurdistan. I speak Kurdish, Farsi [Persian], and a little Arabic, and am now learning English.

My family is still in Iran. I had to leave because my father was put in prison three times for working on Kurdish matters. I am happy to be here; I feel safe, but I am worried about my dad, my mum and my sister. I have no news of them; they do not have a telephone, so I don't know if they are OK or not.

Kurdish people have a bad time in Iran. Like many Kurdish people there, I never went to school, where you have to learn in Farsi and people treat you badly. My father told me not to speak Farsi, only Kurdish. So I can't really read or write. I also had another problem that made it difficult for me to go to school; I have epilepsy. I used to have to go to the doctor every month. I wasn't allowed to go anywhere alone in case I had a fit. So I stayed at home, played football, tennis and other sports. When I had to leave the country, my family paid for someone to go with me. I went to Istanbul first, where I spent three months. Then I came here in a lorry.

Learning English was difficult for me at first, as I was learning a new language and also learning how to read and write for the first time. But I would like to be a teacher myself one day, to help others learn these skills.

Apart from worrying about my family, I am happy here. I have made many friends, including some from other parts of Kurdistan. It is good to be able to walk down the street and know that nobody will ask me who I am, whether I am Kurdish, what I am doing here. I feel safe; it is like being reborn. ∎

Jolly Kwigize

Uganda

"25 April 2003 is the day that I will never forget. I was at work when I heard my phone ringing. I could hear the voice of someone I had once loved... When he said who he was I fainted for a while."

SOMETIMES I WONDER what my life would have been like if I had stayed in Uganda. I had my parents, my children and my family around me and I was happy, working as a catering assistant. But my husband is from Burundi. When he finished studying he could not get any work in Uganda so he went back to Burundi to set up our matrimonial home. He was caught in the war there and imprisoned on suspicion of collaborating with the rebels. We had no contact with him for two years while he was in prison. No one knew where he was. We heard that he might have been killed in prison.

I didn't show the children my misery about their Dad but whenever they asked me I shed tears. I had lost hope of ever seeing him again. Because of what was happening in Burundi I knew that my husband was no longer there for me. This was the most difficult time I have ever experienced in my life.

25 April 2003 is the day that I will never forget. I was at work when I heard my phone ringing. When I picked it up, someone talked and asked me if I was Jolly. I said yes. He coughed and cried for a while without saying anything. I was confused but could hear the voice of someone I had once loved. When he said who he was I fainted for a while.

Then we carried on talking. He told me how hard it had been but that a friend had helped him escape to England.

He eventually got permission to stay in the UK and we joined him in September 2005. Our youngest son had never seen his father and called him 'uncle'. I was very happy to see my husband but I also felt sad, especially saying goodbye to my mother.

Life in Oxford was very different. I stayed indoors because of the cold and prayed hard to get used to the situation. I saw snow for the first time, looking like white flies. The children complained about the cold and about having to be indoors so much. In Oxford everybody is out working during the day and it's hard to make friends. All the time I felt like going back to Uganda, but my mother had told me to be firm and trust in God who holds the future. I went to Refugee Resource for help.

Now I am happy. My children go to school and I work as a catering assistant at Cheney School. I love my job and, because I'm earning some money, I can talk to my mother on the phone and send money to help her. But I always wonder what the future will bring. ■

Bledi

Albania

"There are a lot of opportunities for the future here in England, which is good for very ambitious people like me."

HI. MY NAME is Bledi. I come from Eastern Europe and I speak Albanian. I was the only kid of my parents.

I arrived in England over three years ago on Christmas Day 2002. I was only 13. I have been studying ever since. First I started at Donnington Middle School, then I moved to Oxford Community School where I am still studying now. I concentrated a lot on my English at the beginning and I caught up very fast with the other students. Very soon after I arrived I made a lot of friends which was lucky for me. I then chose the ones I wanted to spend more time with after I got to know them a bit better.

My life has been fairly good since I have lived here. The system in this country is very good and so are most of the people I've known. There is not much pollution here but I do miss the weather in my country. There are a lot of opportunities for the future here in England, which is good for very ambitious people like me. I will carry on studying, preferably business and economics, at university, although I also like cinematography. My favourite kind of films are mafia, romantic and comedy. I like music too. I listen to trance, pop, classic, dance classics and a lot of '80s music. A bit weird for my age, the last one, and so is the next. I dislike rap and hip hop. My teacher always says: 'You should have been born 20 years ago and listened to those songs when they were released for the first time.' I say: 'Then I would have liked '60s music!'

I like wearing smart designer clothes and I would like to drive a Mercedes – when I get my driving licence.

I am reliable and I've got a strong character but am also very sensitive. People trust me. I am physically well built, with wide shoulders, but not very tall. I like to go camping and sailing. I also go to the gym and the swimming pool. I've got a certificate in canoeing and I've finished a DJ course.

That's the sum of my life. ∎

Micheline

Congo

"We came here with someone who put us on a bus to Oxford. We didn't know anyone here; we didn't have any money and we didn't speak any English. So when we got to the bus station we waited until we heard someone speaking French."

I CAME HERE from the Congo with my sister Nanou four years ago. I was 17 at the time and she was 15. We came here with someone who put us on a bus to Oxford. We didn't know anyone here; we didn't have any money and we didn't speak any English. So when we got to the bus station we waited until we heard someone speaking French. They introduced us to a friend of theirs from Congo Brazzaville and said that we could stay one night with them.

The next morning we went to Social Services. They said we would need to see immigration in London but in the meantime found us somewhere to stay, and gave us some basic things we needed. It was an enormous house and we were the only people there. My sister was afraid to stay in such a big house and we slept in the same room.

The next day we went to a smaller house. We enrolled at school; she went to Oxford Community School and I went to English classes. We got a lawyer. We did lots of window-shopping! I didn't want to be alone in the house and neither did she, so we made sure we went home together each day. We still needed interpreters to go to the doctor, but I wanted to learn quickly. I used to carry a dictionary with me to look up words and phrases. At first my sister wanted me to do all the talking, but with the encouragement of her teacher she soon started to learn English as well.

In the four years we have been here, we have been moved six times, sometimes with no notice at all. It was very hard for us. We were living in a house with holes in the floorboards and which had a hole in the roof which dripped water into the living room. One day I came back to find my sister crying and crying. Water was pouring in. I had to pretend I wasn't upset; to be strong for her. But it was hard. We spent another four months in that house, despite many people writing to try and get us moved. In the meantime I had a daughter, Yasmin.

Meanwhile the war in the Congo continues. We have no family there any more. What would we go back to? There are things that happened there that it is impossible to tell you. The scale of poverty; the war, the children living on the street. All the people waste their suffering for nothing. Congo has its own riches but the people don't benefit.

Now I volunteer at a playgroup on a Friday. I am going to do a childminding course. I want to work in a hospital to help with sick children. My sister hopes to do a care assistant's course. We want to study. I would like my daughter to study too, like her mother. I want her to have an intellectual basis on which to build her future. It is this I hope for. I don't care about money. If I had two pounds to spare, I would send it back to the people in the Congo who are suffering so much. ∎

Fidelis
Kenya

MY NAME IS Fidelis. I am 18 years old and am studying Advanced Health and Social care in Oxford and Cherwell College am hoping to go to university after my course. I am Kenyan: half Kikuyu and half Maasai.

I came to England two and a half years ago and I now live in Oxford. I have a boyfriend whom I met here and he is English, we love each other and we hope to be together someday.

I like this place but I miss home a lot. I'll visit one day, God willing. Thanks! ∎

"I like this place but I miss home a lot, I'll visit one day, God willing."

Filda

Uganda

MY NAME IS Filda. I came from northern Uganda in 1989. I have been here now for 17 years. I came with my daughters, but I lost my husband. I have worked for Asylum Welcome and have founded BK LUWO, a Ugandan community women's group based in East Oxford. I have many friends here in Oxford. But I miss my country. ■

I miss my country.
I miss the spacious fertile land where anything grew, giving an abundance of free fruits, vegetables, cereals, and pulses just at the price of one's labour.
I miss the varieties of affordable organic food in the village market.
I miss the open fire, with young people singing, playing instruments and dancing and the lively Sunday church services.
I miss the weather; the sunshine and the red red earth.
I miss the time when everybody helped everybody else.
I miss the abundant cool spring water, at the cost of bringing it home.
I miss my farm and my animals, my banana trees, my sugarcane, my orchard.
I miss the river that bordered my farm land, where my children swam;
I miss the flat clean rocks on which I dried my cassava and did my washing and where we would sit and watch my son and husband fishing.
Above all, I miss the belly laughter that doubles you up; African laughter which there is no stopping. You do not laugh our laughter.
If there were no guns, my country would be a paradise.

"I miss the belly laughter that doubles you up; African laughter which there is no stopping. You do not laugh our laughter."